PUSHKIN'S FAIRY TALES

PALEKH PAINTING

WORKS OF PALEKH ARTISTS IN THE COLLECTIONS
OF THE STATE RUSSIAN MUSEUM AND ALL-RUSSIA MUSEUM
OF ALEXANDER PUSHKIN (ST PETERSBURG)

RUSLAN AND LUDMILA

RUSLAN AND LUDMILA

PART I

At the seashore's a golden chain;
That golden chain entwines an oak.
A learned cat around that oak
Day and night keeps his walk:
Goes to right—a song he sings;
Returning, left—a tale he brings.

There fauns in woods wander;
there, on trees,
Nymphs are sitting at their ease.
There, on paths where no one's been,
Are creature's traces that no one's seen.
There stands a hut on chicken's feet

Without a window or door in it.
The woods and fields are full of wonder;
There at dawn waves break and thunder
On a somber, sandy shore and, dolesome,
Thirty knights, all young and handsome,
Emerge from water, full of glee,
Led by their Uncle of the Sea.
There a Prince, while passing by,
A king doth capture on the sly.
Over fields and over sea
A wizard carries o'er the clouds
A hero-knight in sight of crowds.
Alone in a tower a Princess stays;
Her commands a faithful wolf obeys.
Grandmother Yaga all alone
With mortar stepping all along.
King Kashey pines over gold abundance—
There Russian spirit—Russian fragrance!
I was there; mead there drank;
Beneath the oak reposed on the bank.
The cat to me his tales hath told—
Many tales and tales of old.
One of these I still remember:
This to the world I will render.

Things of days long since passed,
Traditions of a hoary past.

With his powerful sons and friends
In his high hall of audience,
Vladimir-Sun caroused.
His youngest daughter he espoused
To the fearless Prince Ruslan;
And with heavy glasses clinking,
To their health mead was drinking.
Slowly our ancestors dine:
Slowly 'round doth grope
With the foaming beer and wine,
The ladle and the silver cup.
Into their hearts joy's stream is pouring;

Д. Буторин с Палех 1934

Goblets, hissing over brims, tarrying
Cup-bearers are gravely carrying.
Slowly around they go
And to the guests bow low.
The speeches of the guests, sitting 'round,
Merge in one confused noise.
Suddenly a singer's voice
Is heard, and a dulcimer's quick sound.
All are silent, listen to Bayan:
He praises, sage divine,
Ludmila's beauty, Ruslan,
And the wreath which Lel did twine.

Worn out by passion, tired, irate,
He did not drink or eat, the infatuated
Ruslan. His friend he admired,
His moustache pulled impatiently:
Each moment he did count.
Behind the table round,
Three knights sat silently
Before an empty ladle...
Forgot the cups completely,
The victuals were not desirable.
They rivals were of Ruslan.
They heard not eloquent Bayan,
Their eyes to earth were cast.
Unhappy guests!
Concealed deep in their breasts
Are grief and love and hate.
One, Rogday, a daring warrior,
Whose stern sword the Kiev frontiers
spread,
The other, Farlaf, savage clamorer
At banquets, never conquered,

Indolent lord amid the swords.
The third with passion burned:
The Khozar Khan Ratmir.
All pale and stern
Unhappy, at the feast appeared.

The banquet over, they rise in rows,
The guests, and mingle in crowds;
Make obeisance, greet the newlyweds.
Her glance the bride to earth hath cast,
As though her heart were sad.
The groom is radiant and bright.
The shadows on the earth have spread
And close the hour of midnight.
Drowsy with the wine, the boyars bow,
And to their homes begin to go.
The groom, in passionate intoxication,
Is, in his imagination,
The beauty of his bride caressing.
With concealed sad feeling
The Grand Prince his blessing
To the young pair's giving.

And now the young bride is led
To the waiting nuptial bed...
In the stillness of the night
Lel the lamp did light.
Fulfilled is the charming hope!
Ruslan is ready with the gifts of love to cope.
The jealous clothes drop on the bed,
Upon the Tzargrad carpet.
Dost thou hear love's whispers?
Sweet sounds of the kiss
And broken murmurs and caresses
Of the submitting bashfulness?

The groom beforehand hath
experienced delight—
And here it is in sight...
Suddenly a thunder clap sounded!
A light flashed through the mists;
All things hath bounded.

The fire was suddenly extinguished,
Darkness all surrounded.
And all again was quiet.
The heart sank in Ruslan, astounded.
In sinister silence of the night
Twice was a strange voice heard.
Someone with smoky darkness covered
As the mists above the earth
Hath for an instant hovered,
And disappeared in darkness of the night.

The chamber again was empty and quiet.
He rose from bed, affrighted husband!
From his face rolled perspiration.
Trembling, his cold hand
Implored the darkness in his agitation.
Alas! His friend no more the chamber graces!
But empty air Ruslan embraces.
Ludmila in the chamber was no more—
Carried away by a mysterious power.

If one, a martyr, suffers in some fashion
From stirring love and hopeless passion
Though life be lonely and unkind
To him, still life endurable he'll find.

И ЛЮДМИЛА.
С. ПАЛЕХ В. ЕРОХИН 1936.

But after many years
To embrace a beloved friend—
Object of desires and tears—
And suddenly see her disappear,
Forever taking leave...
My friend, I rather would not live.

Yet, he's alive, our Ruslan, the unfortunate.
But how greeted him the
Prince disconsolate?

Distraught by ominous gossip, full of ire,
Of his son-in-law he doth inquire:
"Where is Ludmila? Where is thy bride?"
Ruslan's blushing face
Betrayed the anguish of disgrace.
"Children, friends," said the Prince,
"I well remember your past service.
Have ye pity on me.
Who will ride the Princess to regain?
His deed will not be done in vain.
To him (endure thou cruel torture,
murderer,
Who could not of a wife take care!)
To him I'll give the Princess for a bride
And half of my kingdom, beside."
"I," said the groom in fear,
"I—I—" called with Rogday,
Farlaf, and the happy knight, Ratmir.
"We will our horses gird
And ride all over the earth;
We will not stay away,
We shall not delay.
Father, have no fear:
Soon with thy daughter we'll reappear!"
With silent gratitude, the wretched
Man to them his hand outstretched.

All four together are leaving.
Ruslan is somber, despondent and grieving.
Memories of his bride
His mind doth chide.

All mount their spirited horses,
And along the happy Dnieper's shores
Are soon flying, whirling dust
And in the vague distance are lost.
But long the Grand Prince
Stood gazing into the distance,
The dismal distance after them was eying,
His saddened thoughts after them flying.

Ruslan, tormented, silently
In a maze of memory was lost.
Looking backward haughtily,
With arms akimbo, weightily
Farlaf rode behind our Ruslan;
Said, "I with much difficulty ran,
My friends, away to this fight.
Soon will I the giant put to flight.
O victim of a jealous mood,
I'll soon be shedding thy blood!
Be merry, mettled horse,—
Be happy, faithful sword!"

The Khosar Khan is certain in his mind
Ludmila he will surely find.
Ludmila he in thought embraces...
On his saddle well nigh dances;
In him seethes the bold, young blood.
He gallops impatiently on the road.
Full of hope are his sparkling eyes,
And teasing his bold steed,
And, whirling on, full speed
Up the steep hills he flies.

Stern Rogday not a word is saying;
Silently his plan he's laying.
Affrighted by uncertain fate,
Tortured by the pangs of jealousy,
More than the others he's irate,
And oft a glance well filled with hate
His somber eyes does animate.

The rivals to the same road keep,
All day together ride.

Darkness shrouds the Dnieper deep,
'Twixt misty sloping shores
the Dnieper courses.
From the east creep the shadows
of the night
'Tis time to stop and rest their horses.
And here their path is crossed
by another road.
"Time to part," the riders say.
"Blind fate we will implicitly obey.
Let's suffer her for us to bode."
Each horse then feeling no spurs,
Took for itself its own road.

Unhappy Ruslan, how dost thou fare
Lonely in the desert silence?
His own wedding night to our Prince
Appeared like a hideous nightmare.
Over his brow his helmet pulled;

The reins he dropped from powerful
Hands. Trotting with slow pace,
He saw hope die within his soul,
Disappearing, leaving no wake, no trace.

Suddenly, before the knight
Appeared a cave; within the cave a light.
Beneath the sleepy vaults he doth ride,
Caverns old as earth and tide.
Despondently walks in, the knight. ...
What beholdeth our Prince?
An old man serene, a tranquil glance,
Of peaceful mien, calm appearance.
A lamp before him burning,
And leaves of old books he is turning,
Attentively is reading thereon.
"Welcome, my son!"
To Ruslan, smiling, he is saying,
"Twenty years alone
Here, I was praying
To meet thee. Yea,
Here, in old age, in darkness fading,
At last arrived the day.
A long time I was waiting—
We're bound by fate! Stay,
Sit down here and abide...
Ruslan! Thou hast lost thy bride.
Thy doom art fearing;
Thine ardent courage is disappearing.
But thy cruel grief will vanish fast—
A short time only will it last.
With hope and happy faith
Meet everything. Thy glorious fate
Will at no time thee betray.

Have no fear when thou from here
dost part.
Forward, with thy sword and fearless
heart!
At midnight make thy way.

"Know, Ruslan: The midnight raider
of thy place,
Seducer of maidens beautiful of face,
The horrible enchanter, Chernomore,
Who the midnight mountains doth rule.
No one his castle ever did explore;
But thou, destroyer of all cruel
And evil wiles, will enter there.
And he, the crafty murderer,
Will perish at thy hands.
I will say no more to thee...
But be assured: Good cheer awaits thee."

The knight fell at the feet
Of the sage; grateful, kissed his old hands.
His eyes again with hope were lit.
His heart forgot its torments;
His spirits revived. But soon mortification
Lighted up his face.
"I know the cause of thy vexation.
Happily 'tis easy to efface,"
The old man said.
"The sorcerer's love for the maid
Is loathsome to thee. Be thou at rest,
today.
It is no longer fearsome. He may
The stars in the sky assemble,
Or whistle and the moon will tremble;
But against the law of time,
Futile is the power of his crime.
Jealous, trembling and dour,
Custodian of his castle's doors,
All his wiles are without power
Against the captive he adores.
He wanders 'round the maid
And is cursing his cruel fate...

But, good knight, the day hath passed—
'Tis time for thee to rest."

Ruslan on soft moss doth creep
Before the dying fire, to sleep.
Tired, he lies down, sighing, shifting,
Seeking his own mind to rest;—
In vain. The knight, at last,
To the old man his eyes uplifting,

"I cannot sleep, father! See
My sleep brings no rest to me.
What shall I do?—My soul is ill,
Wearied of life I feel.
Suffer me to revive my heart
With holy conversation.
Confess! Tell who thou art!
Forgive audacious interrogation,
Mysterious enchanter blessed:
Why did you here in the desert come to rest?"

The old man sadly smiled and sighed
And thus to our knight replied:
"Courteous son! My country distant
Long I did abandon,—'tis a somber land.
A native Finn I am. In truth,
In blessed, carefree youth
Through its valleys I did rove;
The herds of neighbours—villagers I drove;
I knew naught but thick forests, swift
Streams, the caves of our cliffs,
And poverty's tempestuous diversions.
But now it grieves—I wince—
To make this painful, grim assertion:
To live in comfortable quiescence
I have not been permitted since.

"Then in our village,
Like a solitary flower, here
Lived Naina, reputed far and near
For the beauty of her image.
One morning when the sun began to climb,
I prowled o'er dark meadows with my herd
Blowing a bagpipe to a rhyme.
Around me the roar of the waterfall I heard.
A youthful maiden on the shore
A garland of flowers twined.
'Twas fate that brought me to her, I opined.

O knight, she was Naina...
I drove my herd and closer came;
And love's fateful flame
(Which since I grieviously deplored)
For my audacity was the one reward.
I then discovered love—its heavenly bliss
And its cruel miseries.

"Slowly, half a year went past;
And, trembling, I confessed my love at last.
My timid sorrow she heard;
Proud and unconcerned, she said:
'I do not love thee, shepherd.'

"All became wild and blurred.
I took aversion to oaks and shadows,
To the diversions of the happy shepherd,
And no consolation could I find.
Dejected, I at last had steeled
And forced all thoughts in my mind
To leave my native field:
The treacherous and stormy deep
With daring throng to sail across,
Military glory to reap,
Proud Naina's attention to engross.
I called for daring fishermen
In quest of gold the sea to span.
Then, for the first time was heard
In my country the sound of the sword
And the shouts of roving seamen.
Ten years the waves and snowy seas
We reddened with our victories.
Our fame grew. Tsars of distant countries
Feared my fearless crew. Their proud hordes
Fled from the northern swords.
Long and joyfully we fought
Tributes and gifts dividing as we ought.
And oft sat with our conquered
At a joyful friendly banquet.
But a heart enchanted by Naina's memory,
Amid the noise of banquets and of victory,
Secretly and long was yearning
To Finnish shores to be returning.
'Time to return home now, my friends,'
I said, 'and hang our idle quivers
Beneath the roof of native shanties.'
Oars grew noisy on the rivers,
Leaving in our wake foul fear.
Proud and joyful in our native bay again
We did appear.

"Fulfilled my dreams, my ardent desires!
The scene of joyful meeting
I beheld with my own eyes;
And at the feet of the disdainful beauty,
I laid my bloody sword,
And corals, diamonds, all my booty
Spread o'er with passionate word.
Silently, stand near
Her envious friends.
I stand, a captive drear.
Indifferent to my lot,
She departed unconcerned,
Saying in a voice so stern—
'Hero, I love thee not.'
"How shall I then narrate
My son, what to relate
I have no more strength?
E'en now, at present moment,
With lifeless soul at threshold of the grave,
The memory of that mortification,
I cannot brave.

Whene'er this somber scene appears,
On my beard roll bitter tears.

"In my somber land
Among the desert fishermen
Is hidden a secret science.
Beneath the vault of eternal silence
Amid the woods and distant thickets
Live gray old magicians.
To things of wisdom they direct
Their thoughts and their emotions.
All things their wisdom knows:
What passed, and what shall come again;
Each thing before their stern will bows,
And over love and death they reign.

"I, searching ardent love,
In hopeless sorrow strove
Naina to attract with aid
Of sorcery; in the heart of the maid
Enchanted love to light.
I hurried, in embrace of freedom,
Into the solitary dark of night.
In the woods with their wisdom,
Many years I passed. ...
The day arrived at last
When I discerned the mystery
of adjuration—
The crowning consummation
Of my love's aspiration.
'Now Naina, thou art mine,'
I said within my mind.
But in truth fate alone did conquer—
Fate, my relentless haunter.

"With dream of youthful expectation,
In an ecstasy of desire
I performed, in haste, an adjuration,
Spirits of dark woods inspired.
A thunderous arrow flashed;
A howl of enchanted storms arose;
The earth beneath my own feet crashed;
And suddenly I saw sitting close
To me, a decrepit old woman, gray-haired,
Hunchbacked and with trembling hand,
Sunken eyes sparkling bright:
Of somber degradation a sight.
That was Naina, courteous knight!
With my eyes I viewed the sight
Of this ghost, and I doubted what I saw.
Suddenly I screamed and cried:
'Is it possible, Naina, thou ?
Where is thy beauty?
What hath chanced to thee?
Did fate change thee so horribly?
Is it so long since I, all hurriedly,
Took leave of our world for my quest?'
'Forty years have passed,'
The maiden made reply.
'I am seventy today—alack!
What shall I do?' she squeaked.
'My years swiftly flashed by—
Thy spring passed; mine, too, did pass.
Both of us have grown old, I profess;
But, my friend, no harm forsooth

To lose the faithless youth.
Certainly my head is covered with gray hair;
A little hunchbacked am I, not so fair
But—the chatterbox then added—I confess—
Thy Naina is a sorceress.'

"Her words were true.
With all my enchanting virtue

I stood a simpleton near her
And this made me more hapless: my vaunting
Came true, to my own terror.
My goddess was me now with her love haunting.
Ugly lips in a smile twisting,
In her squeaking voice this old inelegance
To me love's words was whispering.
Think what a sufferance!
With eyes cast to the earth
I listened to her passionate words.
'Thus did I discover,
My friend, I'm thine forever.
With tender passion I burn;
Desires of love I suffer.
Come thou to my embrace; I yearn
For thee. O love, my love, I'm dying.'
Meanwhile, dear Ruslan,
With love she was me eying
And unto my kaftan
With emaciated hands was hanging,
While I was almost fainting.
This I could no longer stand:
I broke away. And with all my strength
I ran. 'Thou undeserving,'
I heard her harsh voice raving,
'Thou my name hast stained.

Thou hast disturbed an innocent maid's
Restful days.
Naina's love thou hast gained
And now despise! ... Those are the ways
Of all men! They breathe with shame!
Alas, I have myself to blame.
He seduced me, the poor unfortunate!
I submitted to his love passionate!
Betrayer! Monster! What a shame!
Now fear me, seducer, defamer
Of a maiden's name!"

"Thus we parted. Since that separation
Sorrowful, I live in solitude.
And now my only consolation
Is but nature, wisdom and serenitude.
Now only the grave do I await
But her strong love does not abate
For me and her flame of love, of late
From spite hath changed to hate.
With a dark soul thus loving evil
The old woman most certainly
Will haunt thee.
But sorrow is not eternal."

Avidly is listening the knight.
His eyes are bright,
He is awake—he sleeps not—
Hears not the flight of night.
Erewhile the radiant day the world doth grace,
With a deep sigh the grateful knight
The old enchanter doth embrace;
And then, with his soul once more hopeful,
Takes his leave... With his feet spurs
The neighing horse
And whistles, on the saddle turning.
"Father, do not forget me."
The old sage to his friend
His good wishes is returning.
"A happy journey! Forgive me;
Love thy wife; be wise.
Forget not an old seer's advice."

PART II

Rivals in the art of war,
Devoid of peace shall be your fate.
Pay tribute evermore to glory,
Get drunk with hate.
Astound the world with bloody victory—
No one shall dare to interfere.
But rivals of another sort, ye knights
Of Parnassus mountain, pray hear:
Your quarrelsome verbosity excites
Only jeers. Quarrel—but remain
Ye ever dignified until the end.
Ye rivals for a maiden's hand
Remain ever truthful friends.
Trust me: he for whom the gods did ordain
A maiden's heart, he will charming remain
All the world to spite.
'Tis but sinful and foolish to fight.

An ominous foreboding hath oppressed
Untamable Rogday.
Leaving all his fellow wayfarers, he pressed
Forward on a solitary way.
He rode along the woody desert
And by furious thoughts was he stirred.
Cruel spirits thus infuriated him.
The stern knight to himself was
whispering,
"I'll kill... I'll murder him.
Oh, how the maiden must be crying."
His veering steed full speed was flying.

Meanwhile, valiant Farlaf was
in the embrace
Of peaceful dreams and fleeting.
Hiding from mid-day rays
At noon beside a brooklet he was eating,
His spiritual strength thus fortifying.
Suddenly he saw a knight across the field—
As though a cyclone to him flying.
Forgetting quiver, spear and shield,

And leaving his enjoyable repast,
Farlaf, aghast,
Leaped on his saddle; fearing backward
To cast his glance,
heedlessly was flying.
"Wait, low coward,"
The other was crying
After him. "Suffer me to tear
thy head away."
Farlaf recognizing Rogday,
Shriveling and fainting in his fear,
Thought he saw death near,
And his horse still faster he was driving,
As might a hare, who, striving
To run away from dogs, is keeping
Ears down, leaping
Over hillock, field, with all his might.
Nearby this glorious flight,
Muddy streams did flow,
Swelled by the spring's melted snow,
Into the wet breast of earth digging.
Waving his tail, the mettled steed,
To the turbulent ditch came full speed;
Biting his bridle, over the slope
And over the ditch the horse did lope.
But the timid rider, feet up,
Heavily fell into the dirt
Seeing neither sky nor earth,
Already cruel death he was embracing...
"Perish, coward!" His stern sword raising,
Spoke Rogday, but soon did recognize
Farlaf and dropped his hands, distressed.
Disappointment, rage, surprise
His features then expressed.

Gnashing his teeth, and without speech,
Our hero rode away with bent head,
From the ditch.

Then beneath the mountain
an old hag,
Gray-haired and hunchbacked,
With crutch pointing to the north:
"Thereto," she said, "go forth.
There wilt thou find him."
Joyful, filled with renewed vim
To meet his certain death, Rogday
Thence to the north rode away.

Farlaf, left in the ditch,
Marveled in his fear:
"Where did my rival disappear?"
Suddenly he heard the voice
of the witch:
"Rise, brave knight, thou art free.
I have brought thy horse to thee.
Rise and harken to me."
Confused and startled rose the knight;
Crawling, he left the muddy ground.
Timidly he looked around
And sighed, but his spirit again revived.
"Thank God," he thought, "I am alive."

"'Tis hard to find thy maid,"
the witch did say,
"To a distant land Ludmila ran away,—
Neither I nor thou wilt find her.
'Tis dangerous for thee the world to
explore—
Thou wilt be sorry at the end.
Harken, my friend:
Go to thy homestead near Kiev and
there tarry
In thine own shelter solitary;
In thine inherited home warily remain.
Leave the rest for me:
I will for thee thy bride retain."

Thus saying, she did disappear.
Our prudent hero, overcome by fear,
Took leave of glory, and the Princess' love.
Only for his own home he strove.
The least animation,—
The flight of a titmouse,
Or the water's noise,
Threw him into heat and perspiration.

Meanwhile, Ruslan far off hath strayed,
Into the woods and desert field,
His mind by one thought swayed:
"Where is my joy concealed?
At what place doth she hide?
Where art thou, my bride?
Will I again heed thy speech tender?
Or perchance art thou fated with the old enchanter—
Ever a captive—in his turret to stay?
And doleful maid, growing old,
In a dark cell to fade away?
Then, perchance, an audacious rival bold
Will come?—No! No! My faithful wife,
Not as long as I am alive
And my head yet from my shoulders hath not rolled;
And thank the Lord,
I yet carry my trusty sword!"

Once on a sombrous eventide,
While our knight
Rode along rocks of a steep bank,
Suddenly, behind, he heard a clank—
An arrow whistling, struck his shield.
Then came the sounds of a quiver, and a neighing,
And a thud, rolling over desert field.
"Stand still," a thunder-voice was saying.
And, like a storm in his might
In whirling dust there flew a knight.
The rider called as he rode apace,
"Be ready for a deadly combat, knight,
To lie down, a corpse, in this place,
And find for thee here a bride."
Ruslan recognized the rider savage,
As he shook with violent rage.

My friend! Let us leave our knight,
Nor heed his savage fight.
'Tis time to think of our maiden—of her
And of the horrible Chernomore.
How the hero of my dream, the knight,
Though immodest at times, I narrated,
How in silence of the night
From the beautiful Ludmila was separated;
How Ludmila, from Knight Ruslan, astonished,
Into the air hath vanished...
When the murderer with powerful hand
Plucked her from her faithful friend,
And from her nuptial bed,
And through thick smoke and sombre air
As a cyclone to the clouds he fled,
Disappearing to his mountain lair.
Then perception and her memory failed her,
And in the horrible castle of Chernomore
She, frightened, trembling and confounded,
At last herself found.

I witnessed on one summer day,
A rooster who over the coop held sway,
After a chicken in court he raced
With, sensual wings his friend embraced,
But over them, drawing crafty curves, there hovered,
The old thief of the chicken quarters,

Taking murderous measures in his flight:
As a bolt from the heaven, in the court fell
the kite.
Again he arose;
But in his murderous claws,
He carried away the poor unfortunate:
To his dark crevices did disappear.
In vain, alarmed by his woeful fate,
And overcome with fear,
The rooster called his beloved mate.
He beheld naught but feathers flying around,
Floating on the wind and falling to
the ground.
Ludmila, till the morn did rest
In sleep, by a dull stupor distressed;
By confused horror she was struck.
At last, at dawn, she awoke,
And thrown into fearful agitation,
Still in her passionate intoxication,
She waited for her groom.
Gazing fearfully around,
She was horrified when she found
She was not in her own room.
The unfortunate maid
Upon, a gorgeous feather-bed was laid,
Beneath the shadows of a baldachin;
Tassels, exotic patterns on the screen,
Sapphires, amethysts which gleam,
And like a flame were playing...
Golden pans were spraying
Currents of aromatic steam.

Thank God, I need not espouse
The beauty of the enchanted house:
Long since Scheherazade
Hath done this before me.
But in no bright turret are we content
When we miss there our friend.

Attired in light and simple dress,
Three beautiful maids appeared.
Approaching our fair Princess,
All bowed low in fear.
One maid with silent steps drew near,
And then with pearly garland bound
Ludmila's forehead 'round.
Casting down her glance, modest,
In azure sarafan the other her then dressed.
Ludmila's curls and her breasts
she covered
With veil transparent as the mists
that hovered
On high. The enviable veil a form embraced,
Deserving paradise to grace,
And two light boots did compress
Two marvelous small feet.
The last maid to our Princess
A diamonded belt did submit,
While hidden singers whistled
happy songs.
Alas! Neither rare stones,
Nor the sarafan, nor the rows of pearl
Which Ludmila's form did girdle,
Nor the songs of flattery,
Would make her heart merry.
In vain the mirror painted her fair
countenance,
Her form thus gorgeously attired.
Casting to the earth her doleful glance,
Ludmila was but pining, and so tired.

They who all the truth may heed,
And the bottom of a somber heart
can read,

Certainly know
That when a woman in her woe,
Through tears, on sly, somehow,
In spite of habit and reason, detests
In the mirror her glance to cast,
Her sorrow no longer is a jest.

Ludmila, alone with her woe,
Approaches the latticed window;
Her glance strays
To clouded distant space.
Snowy vales bedecked with shrouds bright,
High towers, peaks of mountains,

Monotonous, somber, white,
Slumber in eternal silence.
Nowhere a curling smoke a roof adorns,
No traveller amid the snow is found;
No joyful hunt, no hunter's horns
In the desert mountains sound.
Only at times there woefully whistles
The storm, rioting in fields;
And rocking at edge of the gray skies,
Naked woods arise.

She covered her face, our Ludmila lorn,
And ran to the silver door.
With song it opened before her,
And suddenly, herself she found in gardens immense,
More gorgeous than the gardens of Armede
Or those where reigned
King Solomon or Prince Taurede...
Tossing, clamouring groves surround the palace,

Myrtles, laurel woods, palm alleys,
Everywhere proud heads of cedars grow,
Golden oranges reflect them below
In the waters.
Amid the hillocks hovers
May's curling breeze,
Which, with fire of spring, breathes.
Amid the enchanted fields
A Chinese nightingale whistles.
Pearly fountains fly
In the shadows of trembling twigs
With joyful noise, to the sky;
And beneath them magnificent statues glitter,
Which as living appear...
Even Pallada's son and Thebes',
Phidius, contemplating these
Would drop, disappointed, at the end
His marvelous, enchanted chisel from his hand.
Breaking 'gainst a marble impediment,
With a brilliant and fiery curve fall
Many a splashing waterfall.
A brook in the woody dimness flows
Scarce twisting dreamy billows.
Amid eternal greenery, here and there,
Brightly sparkles a cool shelter.
Everywhere bright roses flower.
But the maid, confounded,
Is walking and not turning 'round.
This enchanted splendour she would not adore;
The sight of this indulgence is disgusting her.
In the enchanted garden she saunters,
Everywhere she wanders
Giving free rein to her tears;
Her doleful glance she uprears
To inexorable skies.
Suddenly were lighted up her eyes,
And to her lips she puts her finger:
A horrible decision in her mind lingers.
A high bridge above the waterfall
Is spread above cliffs. With despairing soul
Shedding tears,
She comes near,
Upon the water casts her eyes,
She beats her breast and cries:
To drown in the waves she decides...
Still, into the water she will not leap,
But continues to wander and to weep.

My beautiful Ludmila at last tires
Of running in the sunlight;
And her tears she dries.
Weary, on the grass she doth sit,
In her mind a thought: 'Tis time to eat.
Suddenly by shadows of a tent
Ludmila from on high is overspanned;
A splendid dinner before her is laid,
A knife and fork of crystal made.
Amid silence, from the branches
An invisible harp is heard to play.
Surprised, the captive Princess
In her heart does say,
"Away from love, in bondage,
I desire not to remain alive.
O thou, whose passionate homage
Hath me of all my joy deprived,
Know thy ruthless power Ludmila doth defy;

Ludmila knows how to die.
I care not for thy tents,
For thy songs, nor for thy banquets,
I will not eat, nor even hear.
All life I will pine here
Away. I will die in thy gardens, in tears."
Thus she spake,
But notwithstanding all this,
Sat down beneath the trees
From the relished banquet to partake.

Ludmila at last
Is finished with her repast.
The tent takes flight,
The harp, and all else disappear...
Again, as before, all is quiet,
And Ludmila in her tears
From grove to grove alone strides.
The moon, the queen of the night,
in the skies
Appears. Darkness draws near from all sides.
Tired, the Princess on the hill lies.

Suddenly in the air she doth rise,
Carried by a power tender
As a breeze, which in the palace doth
surrender
Her. Setting her down with care
Amid the aromas of the evening roses,
There again on the bed she lies...
Pitifully, sorrowfully, she cries,
And amid her tears reposes.
Three maids again make their
appearance.
They get busy around the Princess,
Her gorgeous attire undress.
But their imposed silence,
and their somber glance
Betray their pity for the maid,
Their powerless reproach to fate.
With tender hands
The drowsy Princess they undress.
Her ladyship
In nightshirt, white as snow,
Reclines in sleep...

With a sign the maidens now
Retire and are seen no more.
Someone quietly then opens the door,
Scarcely breathing, Ludmila
trembles as a leaf.
The momentary sleep takes leave,
Her fingers are cold; and her eyes betray
but fearfulness.
She redoubles then her wakefulness.
Silent, she eyes the distance...
All is dark—naught but deathlike silence,
Only the beating of her heart she hears.
And as if the stillness whispers all her fears,
Suddenly here they are coming...
coming to her bed.
The Princess in the pillows doth hide...
Suddenly—how fearful, indeed,—
A noise is heard. A sudden light
Illumines the darkness of the night.
Proudly stepping, a throng of negroes
With bare sabers glittering,
Decorous, pompous on pillows
A graybeard they are carrying:
A midget hunchback,
Stretching his neck,
They bring in with measured step.
To his shaved head, donned with a night cap,
Belongs the beard.
To her bed he neared.
Suddenly the Princess from her bed
Leaped: the midget's night cap
With a speedy hand she grasped;
A trembling fist she clasped,
And so loudly she screamed
That she deafened all the negroes.
Fearful then, the midget esteemed,
In haste his ears he closed,
More than Ludmila he trembled.
He desired to run, but was entangled
In his beard: fell and almost strangled,
Stood up and fell over again;
and in great horror
Swarms of negroes trampling,
Running, pushing, making noise galore,
On the run the midget catch.
The esteemed midget they fetch,
And they carry him out,
his beard unweaving.
His cap meanwhile
with Ludmila leaving.

But what hath become of our knight?
Rememberest thou the sudden meeting
at night?
Take thy speedy brush, Orlofsky, draw
The night, the combat beneath the glow
Of the moon's flickering light.
The knights desperately fight
With rage their breasts are compressed.
The spears are cast far away;
The quivers stained. In the fray
The swords were shattered.
The shields broken, and their fragments
scattered.

с. Палех И. Баканов. 1933 г

Each other in a fit of vehemence they
embrace.
Their horses, beneath, black dust do raise.
The combatants entwined remain,
As though by device they are chained
To the saddles.
Their limbs with rage come together;
One foe's breast upon the other
Entwined, are torpid growing;
Along their veins flame flowing;
They rock, and at last are growing
Weaker. Suddenly enraged.
Our hero, with his iron hands,
From the saddle his adversary
disengaged;
Above the river him
suspends
And headlong sends
Rogday into the waves.
"Perish!" he doth cry,
"My cruel envier, die!"

My dear reader, thou hast guessed,
Whom Ruslan hath surpassed.
He was the searcher after bloody wars...
Ludmila he was seeking as his bride.
Along Dnieper's shores
Stern Rogday, Kiev's pride,
Then sought the rival of his maid.
He overtook him; but strength,
The votary of war, betrayed,
And Russia's glory, our ancient,
And daring brave, in the desert died.
I heard a nymph Rogday espied
And in her cold fingers carried him away.
Avidly him she embraced,
And with him to the bottom of the river raced.
A long time since,
The Dnieper's shores were portraying
The huge ghost of the knight,
And oft in a dark night, in sight
Of scared fishermen,
Rogday was beheld straying.

PART III

In vain to enviers were ye forbidden,
In vain for friends did I disguise,
My verse! Ye remained not hidden
From the jealous and the angry eyes.
Already a critic, to oblige these,
Asked me a fateful quiz:
Why Ruslan's spouse
As a maiden I did espouse,
As if her husband to deride?
Dost thou here behold, dear reader,
The black stamp of spite?
Tell me, critic,—tell me, pleader,
Shall I really answer thee?
Blush, unfortunate; God be with thee:
Blush—I'm satisfied that I was right.
In modest kindness remain I quiet.
Thou wilt understand, Klimene,
Victim of the wearisome Hymene.
Thy languishing glance thou didst cast,—
A fleeting tear hath thee distressed,
Dropped on my verse, there left its mark.
Thou blushed and then thy glance grew dark,

And thou sighed... understood thy sigh!
Bold man, thy hour is nigh.
Amour with self-willed vexation
Commenced a vindictive conversation;
And thy infamous head
Soon with crown of thorns be clad!

The cool morning dawn shines
Over the crest of the Midnight Mountains.
In the wonderful castle silence reigns.
Chernomore, regretful, in his own chamber pines,
Yawns angrily from his bed. Without a hat,
In his morning gown clad;
Attending to his beard, his mannerly,
Obedient slaves hum.
With bony comb, tenderly
His long curls they comb;
For sake of beauty and of fondness.
To minister his moustache endless,
Eastern aromas they are listing;
His crafty curls they are twisting.
Then, God knows only wherefrom, suddenly,
Into the window a winged snake comes flying
In rings curling speedily, and instantly
Resolved itself into Naina
While, surprised, the throng is eying.
"I greet thee," she doth say,
"Long respected brother.
I knew Chernomore until this day
From whatever talk, gossip uttered;
But irrevocable fate
United us with common hate.
Danger now is threatening thee,
An ill-omened cloud is hanging over thee

And insulted dignity
Is calling for revenge, to me."
With voice of crafty flattery
The midget takes her hand,
And says: "Wonderful maid,
I am thy votary,
To me thy league is dear, my friend.
We will defeat the Finn's plot.
Harken! Dark snares I never feared,
This is my predestined lot:
Not in vain in his enchanted beard
Chernomore delights.
As long as the enemy's sword doth spare
His enchanted long gray hair,
None of the courageous knights
And none of mortals will destroy,—
His a planned decoy.
Ludmila will submit
To me, and Ruslan surely perish."
And the somber witch:
three times she did repeat
"He'll perish! He'll perish!"
Thus she spake, thrice did hiss;
Three times did she stamp at this,
And as a snake on her way
She fearfully then flew away.
Dressed in vestments rich and sportive
And abetted by the witch, Chernomore
Resolved once more
To bring to his beloved captive,
His beard, submission, and his love.
The bearded midget aided by the blessing
Of Naina, set out the court to rove.
Through endless rooms he was passing,
But no trace of Ludmila found there.
He took his guest yet further
Into the laurel wood
And where the rail fence stood,
And at the lake and round the waterfall,
The bridge, and near the arbours tall.
But in no place did he find her trace.
Who would dare describe his fright,

His rage, his roar, his cry?
Enraged, he was oblivious of daylight;
And loud rang the midget's cry:
"Run, slaves, fly,
And fetch Ludmila by and by.
What? Are ye jesting with me?
Are ye detesting me?
Am I no longer feared?
I'll strangle ye all with my beard!"

Reader, shall I tell to soothe thee
What became of our beauty?
All morning in tears she was mourning
And was laughing. Terrible Chernomore
She feared no more.
Only his beard alone she feared.
He was laughable, Chernomore,
And horror never yet did last
Beside a jest.
She rose from bed and dressed
To meet the morning rays,
Unwittingly did cast her gaze
In the mirror to behold her.
Her golden curls she did raise
From her lilylike shoulders;
Her thick hair she admired,
And with careless hand it plaited.
And her last day's attire
In the nook awaited
Her. She sighed, and dressed on the sly,
And quietly began to cry.
Yet all the time while she was sighing,
The truthful mirror she was eying.
With fancies suddenly excited,
She then decided
To try the hat of Chernomore.
No one was there to explore,
The place, and no one her to be greeting.
To a lovely maid of seventeen,
What hat will not be fitting?

Ludmila never yet had been
Lazy to attire. She turned her hat
Upon her brow, on side and also straight,
Then backwards set it on her head
And behold!—A miracle of fate!
Ludmila in the mirror disappeared!
She then turned it the other way again—
she reappeared!
"Very well, Chernomore,"
She said, "Ludmila fears thee no more."
The Princess the enchanter's hat,
Still blushing with great happiness,
Set backward on her head.
Let's return now to our knight!
Is it not a shame
For hat and beard to claim
Attention, and Ruslan to his own fate
For us to leave?

Ruslan, after cruel victory achieved,
Through thick woods was making way,
When suddenly perceived
A wide vale extending far away
Beneath the morning skies' light.
He trembled unwittingly, our knight,
As before him appeared the sight
Of gruesome battlefield. Here and there
Were yellow bones; everywhere
Were scattered armours, quivers: amid the grass
And over the field
Shone there a harness,

There a rusted shield.
In bones of hands, swords were laying
A shaggy helmet, grass overgrown,
And in it was a skull decaying;
A champion's skeleton struck down
To the ground with his horse.
Everywhere were spears and arrows
Stuck into the earth.
Ivy peacefully did all embrace
And naught in the silence of the desert
A whisper did raise.
While the sun's bright rays
From its infinite height
Upon the Vale of Death cast their light.

The knight sighed;
With sorrowful eyes he beheld the sight
Of the field.
"O field! O field! Who over thee spread
These bones of the dead?
What heroes on thee camped?
What mettled horses on thee stamped
In the last hour of the fateful combat?
What sky the prayers heard?
Why art thou covered with the pall of death?
And why, with grass of mute oblivion,
is earth
Around thee girth?—Perchance
One day oblivion will me entrance;
Perchance on a mute hill
One day will be dug a grave for me;
And the loud strings of singers will be still,
And no one will at all remember me."

The field he then explored...
Our hero was in need of a good sword,
And even of a cuirass.—Our knight
Hath been disarmed in his last fight.
He travelled round the fields
Amid the shrubs, forsaken bones,
Amid the heaps of rusting shields,
Swords, helmets, scattered among the stones;

Arms for himself he was seeking...
In the steppe awoke a rumbling and a creaking,
A jangling, and a clanking and a buzzing.
A shield he lifted without choosing.
Found helmets, ringing horns,—but yet no sword.
The whole battlefield he scoured around,
But nowhere was a sword found...
Many swords, but all small and light,—
But no weakling was our handsome knight—
Unlike the knights of this day.
A spear he lifted in his hands—
Something with which to play.
With quiver his breast he dressed,
And further rode along his way.

Over field paled red sundown; and soon
Above the sleepy leas
Spread the smoky fleece
Of the mists. In heaven rose the silver moon.
On a somber pathway thoughtfully abiding,
Ruslan journeyed riding
On his horse. Then suddenly stood still;
As through the mists he beheld an enormous hill,
And heard something snoring terribly...
Nearer he came to the hill... nearer, and he heard
A sound as though the hill was
breathing heavily.
Ruslan gazed at it without fear,
His dauntless soul was undismayed.
But, moving his ear,
The fearful horse grew obstinate;
He shook his head; his mane rose upright.
Suddenly lighted by the moonlight
The hill grew bright;
And gazing through the dark, the knight
Then saw some wonder facing him...
May I describe the scene?
'Twas with a live, masculine head he met;
Enormous eyes were still with sleep
oppressed;
Above him rocked a cast helmet;
The feathers on his dark crest
Like the shadows were they straying,
In a horrible trance
Over the steppe were swaying.
The head, standing there in silence,
Like a sentinel in somber desert,
To Ruslan had appeared—
A misty enormity by some one reared.
Surprised and disconcerted,

Палех

Коноваловы В и К.

The knight resolved to end his sleep.
He rode around the heap
And gazed at it right close.
And with his spear he tickled the giant's nose.
The head opened its eyes and frowned,
Sneezed, and yawned.
The steppe shook; a storm arose;
From the moustache and the brows
And from the lashes rose a flock of owls.
Awoke the silent woods; the dust arose;
The echo sneezed; the mettled horse
Neighed and flew away.
Our knight bold
Scarcely to his seat could hold,
And after him—a thundering noise.
"Whereto, silly knight?" cried a voice.
"Go back, I am not jesting;
If you come once more to me,
I will swallow thee,—
And with thy body will be repasting."
Ruslan despisingly surveyed
The head; his steed with his bridle stayed.
"Why dost thou disturb me?"
The head cried:
"Some guest fate sent to me!
Harken: disappear thou, get away, fly!
I want to sleep, and now it's night
Good-bye!" But the famous knight
When he heard such disrespectful insult
In angry gravity hath called:
"Be silent, empty head!
I heard an old refrain:
'A wide forehead,
But scarce of brain.'
I'm riding on my way,
And make no noise,
But if I charge on thee
You surely will fare worse!"

Then filled with rage,
Constrained with spite,
The head grew savage:
Bloodshot eyes commenced to light
As though a flame ablaze:
Foaming lips were trembling;
From his ears steam was ascending;
And he with all his might,
Set out to blow at the knight.
In vain the horse closed his eyes,
Bent his head, strained his breast,
And through the storm and rain
Strove to keep abreast.
Blinded, struck by fear, he fled again
Into the field to rest.
The knight attempted to turn back,
And once more was beaten back,
And after him with all his might
The head, like a mad man laughing, the knight
With his jeers he did exasperate:
"Stand still knight!
Why art thou running? Wait,
Knight, thou wilt break thy neck.
Fear not rider, come back.
Oblige now; strike one blow,
Before with battered horse you part."
Thus the head with his tongue was chiding.
Deeply in his heart, his disappointment hiding,
Ruslan threatened with his spear
At the head's sneer.
Suddenly at the head's tongue cold steel
He struck full force at one blow...

Blood from the enraged hill
Like a river began to flow...
Gnawing steel and growing pale,
Surprised, enraged, and dazed,
The head upon the Prince gazed...
Thus at times on our stage,
Some poor pupil of Melpomene
Whom sudden whistling doth enrage,
His discouraged mien
Grows pale; he forgets his part;
Head bent, he stammers, trembles;
In face of jeering crowd, he loses heart.
Availing of a chance, in haste
To the head, who with surprise grew
Dumb, like a hawk the champion flew.
With stern arm raised
He struck with heavy glove, full force
The cheek of the jeering head...
The dewy grass did instantly turn red,
And bloody foam upon the ground was spread;
And rocking, the head
Turned over, rolling, jumping,
His cast helmet thumping;
And underneath upon uncovered ground
The champion a shining sword found.
Lighted with great joy, our knight
Caught the sword and to the head outright
With cruel design in his mind, came near,
Bent to cut the head's nose and ears.
Ruslan already swung his broad sword,
When suddenly an appeal he heard:
The head to him was praying.
The sword aside he quietly was laying,
Anger in him dying,—
His heart was subdued with prayers...
Thus ice melts in the valleys,
When 'tis touched by midday rays.

"Thou hast made me wise,"
The head to Ruslan sighs:
"Thy strong arm proved to me.
I have been guilty before thee.
From this day I will be obedient to thee.
But be thou magnanimous, knight,
Have pity on me.
I, too, was once a gallant knight,
In the wars with knights of a foreign land
There never was one who could against me stand.
And I would have been happy,
were it not for one other:
My rival, and younger brother,
Crafty, cruel Chernomore,
Who our family did disgrace.
Born midget with a beard,
My size, since earliest days,
He hated and he feared.
I ever was a bit plain,
Though tall; while he of foolish size
Was like a devil wise,
And like a devil of cruel vein.
Then to my woe
The wonderful beard of my foe
In magic power is attired.
As long as his beard is entire,
He fears no man on earth,
And by no adversary will he be hurt.
Once he said to me:
'Brother, I will to thee a mystery disclose.
To save ourselves from our foes...
I found, in a dark book 'twas expounded,
That behind the Eastern Mount,
By the quiet seashore, hidden under rocks,
Beneath a deep cellar under locks,
Is stowed away a sword.
I learned of late (Witchcraft to me disclosed)
That by the will of hostile fate

This sword one day will be known to us
And it will vanquish the two of us:
Thy head cut off, my beard defeat.
Most urgently we need
To gain that sword the crafty spirit hid.'
'Why dost thou suffer woe?'
I said, I am prepared for this sword to go,
To any far off desert
Even to the very edge of earth.'
I placed a pine upon my shoulder,
And for the sake of advice upon the other
I lifted my cruel brother.
Thus I ventured forth upon the road
With a courageous heart.
I did stride and stride.
Thank God, as if the prophesy to spite,
All things were right at the start.
Behind the distant mountains
We discovered the fateful cellar,
And I demolished it with my bare hands,
And found the sword that had been hidden there.
But, no good had fate desired.
A quarrel then arose,—
I admit there was good cause—
Who should this sword acquire?
We argued; then to curse began,
But in the end
A snare discovered the crafty man.
He was silent, as though his heart had softened.

'Let's not dispute in vain,'
Said, gravely, Chernomore,
'Friendship we may put to shame.
Wisdom councils peace for evermore.
We'll leave it all to fate
To decide. Let both stretch on
the ground,
(What will not invent hate!)
And who first a sound shall perceive
Should the wonderful sword receive,'
He said, and stretched upon the earth.
I lay down beside him.
I heard no sound.
I thought: I will deceive him;
But I, myself, was found
Cruelly deceived. He, faithless, silently
Rose on his toes over me.
He swung the sword...
As a storm whistled the sharp sword.
I had no time aught to behold,
And my head from my shoulders rolled.
My head with the enchanter's power,
Life's spirit hath retained.
My skeleton with thorns overgrown
In a distant country hath remained,
There in dust, decayed, unburied;
But the cruel midget my head carried
Away to this desert land,
And till today I guard it faithfully
The sword thou holdest in thy hand.
O knight! Fate ever guards thee,
Take this sword and God will reward thee.
And if the midget thou shalt meet
by chance,
Then of him take revenge
Of his cruelty and mockery.
I will then be happy this world to leave,
And I will thee thy slap forgive."

PART IV

Every day from sleep arising,
The almighty God I praise
Because now-a-days
Sorcerers no more are snares devising,
And therefore—God be glorious—
Marriages are safe with us.
Their snares now are no longer dangerous
To our wives and marriage laws.
But there are enchanters
Of another sort, whom I despise:
Smiles, blue eyes,
A sweet voice... Friends,
Trust them not, for they are crafty,
And no attention shalt thou grant
To them. Permit you not their poison
to enchant,
And to thee lasting peace our God will grant.
Poetry's celebrated genius,
Singer of the sights mysterious—
Of love, and devils, and the lofty skies;
Eternal habitant of graves and paradise.
Forgive me, northern Orpheus,*
If in my entertaining story,
The lyre of my self-willed muse
In beautiful lies will thee accuse.

My friend, thou hast heard how of old
A murderer from sorrow, a vow uttered,
And to the devil he sold
His soul, and the souls of his virgin daughters.
And then with prayer,
faith and repentance deep,
He found a holy man as comforter;
How he died, and how they fell asleep—
His virgin daughters.
It captivates and terrifies
The scene of these sombre nights,
The sombrous visions, the somber devil,
And God's anger, and the sinner evil,
His virtuous daughter's beauty...
We were moved, for them, to pity,
We cried;
Their jagged castle we espied;
Their quiet captivity we loved,
Their quiet dream...
Deep in our hearts we blessed Vadim.
Their awakening we then perceived,
And on their father's grave
with them we grieved...
Or... is it possible we were deceived?
And forsooth,
Am I telling thee the truth?

The young Ratmir, flying on his horse
Directed southward his course.
He thought: "Before sundown
I'll overtake Ruslan's loving bride."
But the day into night was grown,
And before him the knight
Only distant mists descried
Above the river.

* Zhukovsky Vasily, the foremost Russian poet of the 1810s

Naught but desert space in sight.
The last ray of sunlight
The woody summits painted bright.
Past dark cliffs he did ride
Searching a lodging for the night.
Before him he saw a valley lie;
And above the cliffs a castle rise.
Jagged walls lifting spires to the skies,
Dark turrets at each corner,
And a maid along the wall, all alone,
By sundown lighted, wandered
As though above the sea a solitary swan.
And the maiden's song was scarcely heard
In deep silence above the earth.

Upon the field the darkness of the night,
From the waves the cold wind rose.
'Tis late, young handsome knight,
Hide thyself among us.

Indulgence, rest, thou wilt find at night;
Noise and banquets during day.
Pray, our call answer and obey;
Come to us, young handsome knight.

Thou wilt find beauties bright,
Tender kisses, tender greetings,
Come to us for secret meetings.
Come to us, young handsome knight.
At dawn, at morning bright,
We'll fill thy cup before thy quitting,
Come to us for peaceful meeting;
Come to us, young handsome knight.

Upon the fields the darkness
of the night,
From the waves the cold wind rose.
'Tis late, young handsome knight,
Hide thyself among us.

She's enticing; she is singing,
And the Khan is answering her call;
The Khan already is beneath the wall.
Pretty maidens ring about him
With friendly speech surrounding;
Their captivating gaze,
The maids take not from his face.
In the palace of the hermits gay,
The Khan is entering.
Two maids lead the horse away,
Another takes the helmet winged.
In a nook are stored
The shield and sword,
And the shining cuirass.
One maid the forged steel unlaces.
An attire of indulgence replaces
His stern warlike dress.
The youth then is following
The maids to a magnificent Russian bath.
Smoky waves, from the silver tubs are flowing,
Above the floor are spread.
Cold, gushing fountains splash.

On a dazzling carpet our Khan is lying,
Transparent steam above him is flying.
Half-naked beauties cast their glances,
Full of indulgence,
And with tender silent care,
The Khan ensnare.
They crowd—a playful throng—
One maid over the knight is swaying
Birch branches long,
Aromatic steam she's spraying.
Another, with the sap of the spring roses,
Refreshes his limbs bare,
In aromas floatingly reposes
His dark and curly hair.
Carried away by his rapture
He thinks no more of Ludmila capture.
He no more remembers her.
Overcome with sensuous desire,
He is sweltering,
Passions him inspire,
And his heart is melting.

When he finished his bath
Ratmir, in velvet dressed, sat
To a banquet in a circle of the beautiful maids.
I am no Homer: he alone may praise
In elevated verse the banquets
Of the Grecian bands,
Foaming cups, and noisy camps.
More fitting is for me
To imitate Parni,
With careless lyre to praise
Nakedness within the shadows of the night.
Love's tender kisses, beauty's grace,
A castle lighted by the moonlight.
I see a castle in the darkness of the night
Where the impassioned, tired knight
Overcome, is a dream enjoying.
His head and cheeks are glowing,
His open lips a kiss invite,
He's slowly, passionately breathing,

Maids whose charms of love incite
He beholds in dreams fleeting.
The door opens in silence deep,
The jealous floor creaks beneath
A maiden's hurrying feet.
Lighted by the moonlight she appears
Before him. The winged dream disappears.
Awake... Thou handsome knight!
Awake... 'Tis thy night!
Awake... Thou wilt deplore each moment lost!
She comes near... he abides
In sensuous dreams engrossed...
The cover from his bed glides,
Before him stands the maiden, breathless,
As though Diana, faithless,
Contemplating a sleeping shepherd...
With deep passion stirred,
Overcome, she trembles;
And her head she bends
Over him. Her knees rest
Against his solitary bedstead.
A kiss interrupts the dreams of our knight
In the deep silence of the night.

My virgin lyre, my friend,
Became silent beneath my hand.
Her timid voice no longer wilt thou hear.
Let's leave the young Ratmir.
I dare not continue my song. ...
Ruslan doth demand,
Our attention: Ruslan, the warrior strong,
Ruslan our truthful friend.

Exhausted with his savage fight,
The knight beneath the head lay down,
Enjoying sleep all night.
Erewhile, the bright dawn
Rose on the horizon
With its morning playful rays
Painting gold the shaggy face.
Ruslan mounted his mettled horse,
And like an arrow again sped on his course.

Withered leaves are falling from the trees,
Yellow painting the meadow's grounds.
In the woods the wind with its whizz,
The singing voices of the birds drowns,
Somber mists the naked hills embrace:
Winter is near. Ruslan, on his way,
Courageously doth race
On his horse, on the road to the distant north.
Each day
New dangers he has to face:
Here he contends with a hostile champion,
There with a witch defiant,
Then again with a ruthless giant.
In the moonlight oft he sees,
As though enchanted, dreaming at her ease,
A nymph, enshrouded by the mists,
On the solitary branches sits,
And with crafty smile on her lips

Though saying to him no word
Still with him does flirt.
But, guarded by a secret purpose,
Ruslan God's protection enjoys.
He listens to no voice,
He is distracted by no scene,
Ludmila alone inspiring him.

Meanwhile by the enchanter undetected,
By his hat protected,
In no place espied,
Where does our Ludmila hide?
In the garden she ever saunters
To her friend she wanders
In her dreams; on their speedy wing
She at times to distant Kiev races
And her father and her brothers there embraces;
With her youthful friends, in her imagination,
Mirthful merry-making she enjoys.

With her nurse she does converse,
Forgotten her captivity and separation.
But suddenly all her dreams are gone,
And the Princess again sorrowful, alone,
Captivity has to face.
The infatuated murderer and his slaves,
Day and night her capture frame.
Scour everywhere for her and call her name,
But in vain!
Oft with them Ludmila playing.
In the enchanted woods doth appear
Without a hat there straying.
And calls out loudly, "Here, here!"
All rush at her sound,
But invisible, aside
With silent step she bounds,
And from their hands escapes.
Each hour at different place
Is discovered her instant trace:
Here golden fruit flutter,
And from noisy branches disappear,
There sparkling drops of fountain-water
On the trampled meadows suddenly appear...
"Surely,"—all are thinking
"The Princess is eating now or drinking."
On the top of a cedar, or birch she does hide
Exulting in a few moments sleep at night.

Tears from her eyes are often rolling,
Ruslan's name she fervently is calling.
Overcome with woe and fits of yearning,
At times before the dawn of the morning,
Against a tree she rests her head;
A brief sleep her heart makes glad,
And in the early morning she does stroll
To bathe her at the waterfall...
The midget from his palace stand
Himself once saw: how by an unseen hand
The water was splashed and sprinkled
there below.
In her customary sorrow
She wanders all day long,
And in the evening is heard her song.
Often amid the flowers suddenly is found,
A garland dropped upon the ground:
At times a shred of Persian shawl appears
Or a kerchief wet with tears.

Worn out by the ravage
Of his cruel passion, blinded with rage,
Chernomore was with one thought
engrossed:
Ludmila he would make his own.
Thus the Lemnos,
Blacksmith, while accepting
a bridegroom's crown
From Cytheria, spread
On her path a net,
Uncovering thus to the jeering Gods
Cipridy's tender plots.

One early morning hour
The Princess while at rest within
a marble arbor
Through the trees' swinging branches,
chanced
Upon the flowered meadows to cast her glance
Suddenly she heard one talk:
"My dear, dear bride,"
—and Ruslan she descried—
His features, his figure, his walk,
His face pale, on his hip a wound,
His eyes with tears were bright.
Dismayed and astounded,
"Ruslan, Ruslan!" she cried.
Fearfully her husband she embraced
But suddenly the ghost was effaced,
And the Princess trapped in a net,
Found herself. And from her head
Upon the earth dropped her hat,
And she someone heard rejoice:
"She's mine," roared a stern voice
And Chernomore she then beheld
standing nigh...
The Princess sorrowfully sighed,
Fell unconscious; and wonderful dreams
Embraced her with their soothing wings.

What will now be the end?
A horrible scene alarms!
The enchanter's audacious hand
Caresses Ludmila's charms.
Will he be happy to the end
Of his days? But lo! Here comes a defender
A horn sounds
A formidable foe the midget taunts!
Terror-stricken, the enchanter
Covers Ludmila's head with his enchanted hat
But the horn ever calling keeps
on howling louder,
With defiance the murderer is greeting
Casting his beard around his shoulder,
Chernomore flew away
for the sudden meeting.

With the beard from his helmet flying
(A token of fateful victory),
Swarms of negroes, in a great hurry,
And throngs of timid maiden slaves,
Like ghosts to every place
Ran to hide. Ruslan set out to wander
Through many a proud chamber.
His lovely bride he called
But only the scoffing echo squalled.
Wroth and impatient,
Into the garden he opened the door,
But nowhere he found a trace of her.
He cast his eyes around,
But the castle all empty he found.
He set out searching through the arbours,
And along the river shores,
And along the waterfall.
Ludmila's name he did shout
But no one answered to his call.
The knight was overwhelmed
by sudden fear,
A distressing thought within his mind arose:
Captivity, sorrows,—
Perchance, he threw her into the river...
He bent his head, his mind grew dark;
He turned lifeless as a rock;
Motionless he stood,
in somber thought engrossed.
It seemed that the wild flame of love did grip
Our saddened knight, as if the Princess' ghost
Approached his trembling lip.
Suddenly wild, desperate,
The Prince set out; he rushed
Through the garden, Ludmila's name did shout,

And with his sword all that came
his way he crushed;
From the hills the rocks tore down;
The bridge in the river he was hauling;
The arbour trees were falling—
The whole field he laid bare—
Naught at all would he spare.
A thunderous howl rose from the earth.
The distant hills the thunder heard.
The beautiful countryside he laid waste:
With his stern whistling sword
everything he defaced.
Suddenly a chance swing brought down
Ludmila's hat upon the lawn:
The farewell present of Chernomore.
Witchcraft instantly lost its power,
And Ludmila in her net he espied
He dared not trust his sight!
With a shout of joy he greeted his bride.
He tore at her net,
And kissing her hands and head,
Tears of love and joy he shed.
He called her—but she remained engrossed
In dreams; her eyes and lips were closed.
The sensuous dreams did still entice
The maid. Ruslan dared not take
away his eyes
From her. Passionately he gazed
At her; her young breasts he embraced.
Once again sorrow overwhelmed him.
Suddenly he heard a voice—
The voice of the charitable Finn,
"Take courage, prince; rejoice!
With sleeping Ludmila homeward ride.
With new joy thy heart fill.
Be truthful to love, honour abide.
God's thunder will strike the evil,
And peace on earth will eternalize.
Go with her to bright Kiev,
and there the Princess
Before thee will rise
From her enchanted caress."

Ruslan with these words was brought to life.
He lifted in his embrace his wife.
With his precious weight, his own bride,
He stepped down from the steep height
And into the vale he descended,
Tenderly carrying in his embrace
his friend.

Ruslan, silent, with the midget gray
Behind the saddle rode on his way
To Kiev. Fresh as spring sunrise
Ludmila in his embrace lies;
Her head was resting on the champion's
shoulder.
Tenderly he held her.
Her hair in ringlets the wind was waving.
How oft her breasts were heaving!
And how oft her calm face
Like an instant rose was gleaming!
Secret dreams to her embrace
The image of Ruslan were bringing.
Often on her lips his name was fleeting,
While in enchanted forgetfulness she
was breathing.
He heard her sigh, beheld her tears,
The smile that on her lips lingered,
The excitement of her sleepy fingers.
A long time over vale and mountain,
In bright day and somber night
Journeyed our faithful knight.
But his native land was yet distant.

And while his sleeping wife he bore,
Evil temptation from his mind he was
dispatching.
Was he really but a martyr
And was his wife only watching?
Had he really only in his thought
Found inspiration?
The monk who truly wrote
For posterity this narration,
Assures us truly in that,—
And I believe it. Without sharing,
Sorrowful and coarse is love's enjoyment.
We are happy only when we are sharing
Together our blissful, joyful moments.
The sleep of our faithful Princess
Was different than thine, O shepherdess!
In spring, once, in a solitary nook
Beneath the tree's shadows on the grass,
There I recollect a peaceful brook,
One time, in evening,
Lydia's dreaming,
A shady grove,
My first kiss of love,
Light fleeting, and trembling.
Hath not scattered, my friends,
Lydia's sleepy patience...
But friends, I babble nonsense.
Why should I now recover this memory?
Its enjoyment and the maiden whom once
I did adore
Do not interest me anymore.
My mind is preoccupied now
With Ruslan, Ludmila and Chernomore!

Before him curled a valley
At intervals with spruce grown;
A black crest the round
And distant hill did crown.
Extending high
Above, far into the bright blue sky.
Here the merited steed increased his
prancing.
Before them towered the wondrous head;
upon them glancing
His pitiful, enormous eyes.
Hair like the woods, above high
forehead,
Seemed reaching far into the skies.
From his cheeks, pale as lead,
Life's spirit fled;

His lips were half open;
his enormous teeth were gnashing.
The last day was thus distressing,—
The colossal head already was half dead.
The knight with Ludmila arrived
There with the midget tied
Behind the saddle. "Good morning, Head,"
Ruslan called,
"Thy traitor before thee I hold—
Thy crafty brother, Chernomore,
Thou mayst see once more."
At the Prince's proud word
The head bestirred,
And opened his enormous eyes
As if from deep sleep he did rise.
Horribly he sighed.
His cruel brother in his horror recognized.
A red flame through his cheeks flashed,
His great dying enormous eyes
Their last rage expressed...
In confusion, in deadly tremor,
With bared teeth gnashing
At his brother Chernomore,
With confused reproach he was lashing...
His long sufferance ended,
From his face at that moment
Life disappeared. His breath weakened,
And his glance was extinguished forevermore.
Soon Chernomore and the knight
Witnessed his last death-tremor
And saw him rest in eternal night.
The midget who at the saddle hung,
Feared to breathe and no comment made:
With dark witchcraft's tongue,
Zealously to the devils he prayed.

In the thick woods, amid cool shadows,
An unnamed brooklet flows
And there upon the sand
A bent hovel stands.
With thick pine the slope is crowned,
By a hedge of reeds 'tis fenced round.
The rill with slow waves splashes;
And, dreamily, the reeds it washes.
It seemed as if upon these shores
Peace since creation reigned supreme.
God's world here was so quiet and serene.
Ruslan halted there his mettled horse.
The spreading daylight
The woods and shores of the rill crowned,
With its rays bright.
Ruslan lay his wife upon the ground,
Sat on the meadow then and sighed,
Gazing sorrowfully about,
Suddenly he saw above the river float,
The humble sail of a boat:
A lone fisherman, his net spread
Above the waves. Bending over his oars
He silently approached the woody shores,
To the peaceful hovel drawing near.
On the threshold then appeared
A young maiden. She stood in sunrise,
With her luxurious hair
Loosely streaming in the air,
A tranquil glance was gleaming in her eyes,
Her lovely breast and shoulders were bare,—
All was lovely and captivating in her...
They embraced each other,
Sat down beside the cool water.
And an hour of carefree rest
And of love quite unnoticeably passed
For them. But whom, to his surprise
In this fisherman sitting so near
To him did Ruslan recognize?
The young Khozar Khan Ratimir!
In love and bloody wars
His rival and his comrade!

Ratmir, on those solitary shores,
His military glory and Ludmila had betrayed!
For all time he estranged
The love of a tender friend.

Our hero then approached the hermit.
The other saw the knight and, deeply stirred,
Ran immediately Ruslan to meet.
A joyful cry was heard,
Each other they embraced.
"What do I see?" Ruslan phrased
His surprise. "What compelled thee
in this place to hide,
To forsake all dangers and thy military pride
And the sword which thy courage glorified?"
"My friend," the fisherman replied,
"My soul of military glory is long tired;
'Tis but a vain and ruinous ghost.
All craving for the bloody wars I lost;
Innocent diversion, trust
Thou my word, love and a tranquil grove
On this unperturbed site of the earth
Are now to me a hundred times more worth.
I will pay no more
Tribute to the madness of war,
With true happiness am I blessed.
For the sake of my lovely friend
I have disowned all my past.
And even Ludmila's love I have disdained."
"Courteous Khan, I am glad,"
Ruslan said. " Ludmila is here with me."
"Where is she? With thee?
Permit me to see her...but no!
It will seem bad...

My friend is all of life and joy to me.
She gave me happiness and bliss, and above
All other things peace and her pure love...
In vain they promised happiness
To me the lips of the enchantresses.
Twelve maidens had me adored
And for the sake of her from their happy
castle I fled,
And in these shadows my heavy sword
Laid down, and my shaggy helmet.
All my glory I disclaimed,
I forgave all my foes on earth;
A peaceful hermit I remained
Alone, since in this happy desert...
With thee my lovely friend,
For thou my friend art
The light of my heart. ..."

The lovely sherpherdess calmly
the comrades eyed,
Giving heed to candid talk of friends.
Upon the Khan she reposed her lovely
glance
And filled with bliss, she sighed.

Thus fisherman and knight their thoughts
did share
Till late at night were sitting
On the bank, their hearts laid bare,
Hours unnoticeably were fleeting,
The moon arose. At the approaching night,
All seemed quiet.
Ruslan with a blanket his bride
Covered, and mounted his stout
Steed. The silent Khan thoughtful
followed
After him as in a dream.
For Ruslan lovingly he wished great glory
And happiness and victory;
And with proud memories of his past years,
And at times with a sorrowful thought
His mind was fraught.

Why hath not fortune and fate
My unsteady lyre made
But heroic deeds to praise?
And with it (not yet known to the world)
to relate
Love and friendship of the old days?
Poet of sorrowful truth, O muse,
Why need I to posterity narrate
Evil, secret wiles, and hate,
And the faithless with my song accuse?

Of the underserving contender,
I am narrating
His quest for glory, terminating
Alone, unknown, in the desert stagnating,
Farlaf, hidden; Naina was awaiting.
The solemn hour came.
To him arrived the spiteful dame.
"Go and saddle thy horse,"
She said. And into a black cat treacherous
She instantly was changed.
Farlaf his steed did gird;
Fearfully behind Naina he was going.
Along a somber footpath, into the desert
Wood through dark of night,
he was her following.

The silent vale sleeps
Dressed in evening mists.
The moon in darkness runs about
And hides behind each passing cloud;
And light bright and fleeting,
At times casts upon the mound
Where somber Ruslan is sitting
Near the sleeping Princess stretched
upon the ground.
Over him floats somber dreams
Waiving sleep with their cold wings.
His head is bent over Ludmila's feet,
And gazing at the maid with misty eyes,
Languishing wearily, he sighs.
Over his tired head slumber creeps:
Overcome at length,
beside the Princess he sleeps.
And a prophetic dream the hero sees:
The Princess standing above a precipice
Pale, motionless, overcome with fears.
But suddenly Ludmila disappears.
Ruslan is alone above the abyss,
A familiar voice and sighs
From beneath he hears,
And after his wife he flies.
Then suddenly before him appears
Vladimir, surrounded by twelve sons,
Within a circle of gray-haired champions
In his high hall of audience.
He sees a throng of the invited valiants,
'Round the warlike table all are sitting
And angry is the Prince and still is grieving
As on the day when Ruslan was leaving.
All are quiet; are scarcely breathing—
Daring not the silence to remove.
Stilled is the joyful noise of guests,
And 'round the table doth not move
The foaming cup. He sees amid the guests
Rogday, who in combat was by him defeated,
Alive and at the table seated,
With his foaming glass clinking
Joyfully his mead he's drinking
And heeds not the astonished Ruslan.
Ruslan beholds the young Khan,
And many a foe, and many a friend...
He hears the rapid sound of dulcimer
ringing
And the speech of Bayan, the eloquent,
Who of the heroes' diversions is singing.

Overcome with horror and surprise,
Ruslan suddenly beholds young Farlaf bringing
Ludmila to the hall within.
But the old Prince doth not rise,
His head in sorrow bent,
silently he doth abide.
The boyars and all the princes
Deep in their hearts their feelings hide
And remain in unmoved quiescence.
Suddenly all things are effaced:
Cold death our hero doth embrace,
Fearful, shedding tears, he thinks
That these are naught else
but illusive dreams.
But the ill-omned dreams to end
Alas! already was beyond his strength.

The moon scarcely shines o'er the crests
of the mountains,
The somber wood still darker grows.
Over vale a deadly silence reigns.
The betrayer comes near, riding on his horse.

He beholds a meadow by
the moonlight lit,
He sees a somber mound:
Ruslan sleeping at Ludmila's feet,
His horse trampling around,
Suddenly the witch in mists doth disappear.
Farlaf fearfully draws near.
His heart is beating fast, he trembles,
The reins drop from his lifeless hands.
He unsheathes his sword
And ready is the knight,
To cut in two upon the sward.
The racer scents his foe in fright
And neighs; the ground his foot is breaking
In vain. Ruslan, not waking,
With horrible dreams is distressed
Like a heavy weight those dreams rest
On him. Encouraged by the witch's word,
The betrayer three times plunges his sword
Into Ruslan's heart, pinning him to earth;
And then runs hurriedly, fearfully away
To Kiev with his precious prey.

The unconscious Ruslan all the night
In darkness reposed beneath the mound.
Hours passed. The blood without respite
Was flowing from his inflamed wound.
At morning he opened up his misty eyes,
Painfully, and weakly groaned
With effort he rose from the ground,
Bent his warrior's head
And then again unconscious fell—
without breath.

PART VI

Thou dost command me, my tender friend,
Upon my careless lyre, the legends
Of old times to sing,
And to the faithful muse a sacrifice to bring
Hours of relieving rest.
Lovely friend, thou knowest
From fickle gossip in flight,
Thy friend in beatitudes delights;
Forgot with solitary labour to aspire
The sounds of his precious lyre.
Unaccustomed to exertion, I today
Am with indulgence carried away.
I breathe with glory—and with thee,
Inattentive to the call of my vocation.
The genius of dreams and inspiration
Hath forsaken me,
Thirst of pleasure and love
Alone my heart doth not move,
But thou sayest thou lovest the stories
Of love, tradition's glories;
The champion, Ludmila, thou dost adore;
Vladimir, the witch and Chernomore.
The Finn's faithful sorrows
Thy imagination occupied;
Listening to my gossip light,
With thy smile thou oft wert dreaming;
But thy tender eyes
Yet more tender often on thy bard were beaming.
Thy enraptured friend follows thy advice:
He kneels submissive at thy feet
And his songs for thee he doth repeat
Again he touches idle strings
And of the youthful knight, to thee he sings.
But what have I said?
Yes, what was Ruslan doing?
On the field he's lying dead,
And his blood is no more flowing.
The eager raven over him flies.
No longer does his bright horn sound;
His idle armour's strewn upon the ground,
And upon the earth his shaggy helmet lies.

In a circle 'round Ruslan, the horse
Constantly was keeping course.
Sorrowful, he bent down his proud head,
From his eyes all light had fled.
No longer now his golden mane he waved,
No longer was he frolicking; but grave,
For Ruslan patiently was waiting.
But Ruslan lies unconscious and not waking:
With cold sleep he is chained unto the ground,
And it will yet be long before his shield will sound.

And Chernomore?
In the valley he was left behind
By the witch forgotten.
Sleepy, tired, aware of nothing
Angry thoughts were seething in his mind.
The knight and Princess
He was cursing in his weariness...
At last his heart he steeled,
And stepping out, the countryside was eying.
He beheld the champion was killed
And in a pool of blood upon the earth was lying,
And Ludmila was no longer there...
Only bare and desert field...
The murderer was thrilled!
He believed that he again was free and strong...
But the cruel midget was wrong.
Meanwhile, Farlaf with Ludmila in his embrace,
Along the road to Kiev did race.
Before him the waves of the angry Dnieper raged
Amid familiar pasturage.
The gold-roofed city he very soon was eying...
Already through the city he was flying
On his horse.
A tempestuous noise arose.
People behind the rider did gather
And ran to cheer the heart of Ludmila's father,
The betrayer, becoming bold,
Appeared then at the palace threshold.
Engrossed in woe profound
Vladimir-Sun sat in his turret,
Distressed by somber thought,
Knights and boyars, gravely seated 'round,
Suddenly heard how before the threshold
A loud tempestuous clamour rolled.

Before Vladimir's door,
With Ludmila in his arms stood a warrior.
All, with low whispers,
Rose from their place.
"Farlaf...really...with Ludmila is here'?",
Sorrow vanished from Vladimir's face.
From the chair arose the old father,
And hurried with heavy steps to see
His own unfortunate daughter.
With his fatherly hands
He desired to touch her.
But the lovely maiden was not hearing
In enchanted sleep she was dreaming
In the arms of Farlaf. All were whispering
And all disturbed seeming.
But craftily his finger putting to his lips
Farlaf said, "Ludmila sleeps.
Sometime ago I found
Her in the desert Murom woods on
a greensward,
The captive of a cruel faun.
Savagely we contended with our swords;
Three days gloriously were fighting,—
Three nights the moon
Our bitter combat was lighting.
He fell; and the young Princess at last
Into my hands hath passed.
Who will interrupt her enchanted sleep?
Who will free her from the enchanter's grip?
I know not... Hidden from me the secret
of adjuration.
Patience is for us now the only consolation."
Soon the fateful news was broadcast loud,
And the people, in a motley crowd
In the city market gathered,
a tempestuous rout.
The castle is opened to all.
People are crowding in the hall
Where, on a high bed
With brocaded blanket overspread,
The Princess lies in sleep so sound.
The princes and knights stand 'round

Sorrowful. Trumpets are sounding.
Dulcimers, horns and drums are pounding,
Thundering over her.
The old Grand Prince in despair,
Exhausted by his sorrow,
To Ludmila's feet his gray hair
Lays down with silent tears.
Pale Farlaf is standing near
Disappointed; in his deep repentence,
He casts to earth his glance.
Night arrived, and in the sky the moon did rise;
But no one in the city closed his sleepless eyes.
Noisy crowds in the street were walking,
And about the miracle all were talking.
All the city with excitement was rife;
Even the youthful husband, that night
Neglected his own youthful wife.
But soon as the light
Of the two-horned moon
Disappeared before the morning dawn,
All Kiev was confused by new alarms.
Cries, noises, howls, calls to arms—
All people were crowding the invader to resist,
Gathered for a sanguine fight
At the city walls. Through the morning mist
They beheld tents across the river white;
Like the flames glowed flashing shields;
Riders flying in the fields,
Raising to the skies black dust.
Wagons moving on their heels,
Fires burning on the hills,
Pechenegs are swarming like the locust;
The Pechenegs in a sudden mutiny
The city of Kiev were threatening.
Meanwhile the prophetic Finn,
The Master of the spirits,
Alone in the tranquil desert sits;
And soon the day he hath forseen
Arrived, and the fateful hour came
On earth evil to restrain.
In silent desert, on red hot plains,
Behind a distant chain of desert mountains,
Behind the abode of winds and thunder storms
Where even the witch's daring glance
To penetrate in a late hour scorns,
A wonderful valley lies.
In that vale are two springs:
One, flowing with live waves,
Over stones joyfully rings;
The other with dead water splashes,
Silence there reigns supreme. The wind dozes.
Spring coolness never there the air refreshes
Forever silent, stand century old spruces.
Birds never circle on this spot.
The gazelle in a sultry day dares not
Water there to drink.
Two spirits from the world's beginning
Silent on the bosom of peace there stand:
The shadowy shores they guard...
With two empty ladles in that wonderful land
The hermit comes forward.
The spirits cease their dream and disappear
Overwhelmed by sudden fear...
The hermit then the virgin waters splashes.
Immersing in the springs two glasses,
Into the air then he disappears
And again instantly he reappears,
In that vale at the place
Where Ruslan motionless lies in death's embrace.
The old man bends over the knight,
And him with the dead water sprays.
His wounds grow bright
And beauty wondrous suddenly the corpse
doth grace.
Then with live water again the hero he splashes
And youthful life, Ruslan instantly refreshes.

With a new spirit he doth from the earth arise
And gazes about with his eager eyes.
Like shadows in an ugly dream,
The memories of his past seem
To him. But where is Ludmila? He's alone
In the field. Instantly all joy is gone
From him. But again he is thrilled
with renewed vim;
He hears the voice of the prophetic Finn
Who embraces him:
"O my son, rejoice at thy fate.
A bloody banquet is awaiting thee.
Thy stern sword as a calamity
Will descend upon thine enemies,
And to Kiev thou wilt bring peace.
Ludmila there will appear,
Take this ring and touch her head
Evil charms will disappear. ...
Thy image, among thy foes confusion will spread.

Peace will reign, hate will disappear,
Both of ye deserve great happiness.
Farewell knight. Thou wilt see me no more.
Give my thy hand; we will part forever
Now, for only there, beyond the grave's door
And not before, we will meet again,"
He said and disappeared. Greatly inspired
By his word, with spirit of life fired,
Ruslan raised his hand after him.
But the prophetic Finn was no longer seen.
Ruslan stood alone in the empty field. ...
He climbed upon his mount.
The steed then with the midget still behind
the saddle bound
Impatiently wheeled.
And galloped off, neighing,
With his mane swaying,
And the Prince, alive and sound,
Again flew over field and over mound.
Meanwhile what a shameful scene
Beleaguered Kiev seemed!
Timid sighs in homes were heard:
People overcome by woe,
Were crowding upon the walls that Kiev girth,
Casting their fearful glance upon the meadow.
Grand Prince Vladimir, deserted, alone,
Near his daughter with prayer did moan.

But the courageous swarm of the champions
And the Princes, each with his faithful band,
Were preparing with the foe to contend.
The day arrived!
The hosts of the foe over fields
At dawn advanced from the hills
Upon the city; like a tornado the walls they stormed.
In Kiev trumpets thundered, horns were rung.
The champions in a battle line formed,
And rushed out to encounter the daring throng.
And there they came together on the field!
Scenting death, the horses wheeled,
Sword began to clang on shield;
A cloud of arrows through the air whistled.
The vale with blood instantly was flushed,—
And straight ahead the riders rushed.
The mounted bands intermingled, intertwined,
Close together, in two vigorous walls,
A line there was fighting another line.
There a rider, here a footman was felled
There a scared steed was flying.
Here a Russian was killed;
There a Pecheneg was dying.
Here thunder shouts of war were heard.
And there a host was put to flight.
One was knocked down by a sword;
Another struck by an arrow light;
A warrior beneath a shield was crushed,—
As over him a mad steed rushed.
The battle lasted until dark of night:
But neither we nor foe were put to flight.
That night the champions their eyes did close
Behind walls of mangled corpses of man and horse;
And deep was the sleep on the bloody ground.
Only seldom in the dark of night
Was heard a sorrowful groan
And the prayer of a Russian knight.
The morning shadows were pale.
The waterfall was sparkling with its silvery scale.
A doubtful day was born in the east:
The sun was breaking through the mists.
The morning sky awoke on high,
The hills and woods, grew bright

With sunlight.
But the battlefields peaceful lie,
And mute remained the savage fight.
Suddenly in the foe's camp a cry arose,
The savage clamour of the war's thunder
The peaceful silence tore asunder.
The Russians rushed out in confused rows
And beheld a splendid warrior on a horse,
His armour glowing like a flame.
Like a bolt from heaven he came
To their foes, blowing on his horn,
Cutting, spearing, and flying like a storm.
This was Ruslan; the courageous man
Like a thunder fell upon the Bussurman.
The frightened camp was him descrying,
Galloping with the midget saddled, o'er the field,
Everywhere the angry horse came flying,
Everywhere the stern sword whistled,
Heads from shoulders were rolling,
Wailing rows upon rows falling.

Палех 1949 г.

In one instant the warlike meadows
Were covered with heaps of quivers and arrows,
With hills of bloody corpses
Of crushed, beheaded men and horses.
On the call of war, to the sound of trumpet
Slavic bands mounted,
Came flying over the hills
In wake of our hero's heels.
Horror the Pecheneg embraced. The desperate
Violent children of the raid,
Dared no more resist.
They were calling for their scattered horses,
Wailing, through the fields' dusty mists
They were flying from the Kiev swords.
Victims, sentenced to hell,
Before the Russian sword they fell.
Kiev again was free,
And the Russians celebrated victory.
In the city a mighty champion appeared,
From his helmet waved a long beard.
In his arm he held a shining sword;
Like a star of sky, his spear shone forth.
He was flying, with hope crowned,
Along the noisy streets, to the Princess' house.
The people him surrounded
In enraptured crowds.
Vladimir, by this celebration astounded,
From his silent turret came out,
Sorrowful, overwhelmed by his woe,
He stood there alone. His friends with the foe
On the bloody battlefield were contending;
But at his side Farlaf was standing.
Far from the foe's swords

Far away from the invader's hordes,
He despised the alarm of wars,
And stood guard at the palace doors.
As soon as our hero he did recognize,
His blood turned cold; from his eyes
Light was extinguished; he fell upon his knees.
Deserving punishment he now sees
Is due him for his treachery...
But aware of the powers of sorcery,
The secret charms of the ring,
Of Ludmila in her sleep dreaming,
And the words of the departed seer,
Ruslan with hurried step draws near
Her bed; and with trembling hand on calm face
The charmed ring he placed.
And behold! The young Princess sighs
And opens her bright eyes!
It seemed,
As though oppressed with distorted dream,
She marvelled at such lasting night.
Suddenly she beheld the sight
Of her knight. Ruslan she faced,
And passionately her hero she embraced.
Ruslan awoke with flaming heart;
Tears of joy his woes effaced.
And the Grand Prince, at last solaced,
The lovely ones embraced.

How shall I end my long chant?
Thou hath guessed, my friend.
The unjust anger of the Prince abated.
Farlaf on his knees then truly stated,
Before Ludmila, Ruslan, and before the Prince,
His shame, his crime and his offense.
The happy Prince forgave him.

Shorn of power of sorcery,
The midget in Vladimir's court was taken in.
Vladimir-Sun in his high hall of audience,
Long then caroused with his family, in memory
Of the celebrated fateful victory,
Amid a throng of invited valiants.

Things now long since passed:
Traditions of a hoary past.

EPILOGUE

Thus unconcerned man of society
at my respite
On the idle lap of peace while at rest,
With my obedient lyre I glorified
Traditions of the hoary past.
I was singing—and forgot my ills,
Insults, unhappiness and evils,—
The treachery of Dorida, the unfaithful,
The gossiping of the noisy fool.
Upon the wings of inspiration borne,
Behind the earth I was carried...
Meantime a treacherous storm
Above me spread
And I was perishing. O thou holy supporter
Amid the storm's howl,
Thou, tender comforter
Of my sickly soul,
The stormy weather thou didst entreat,
Thou hast returned peace
to my impetuous soul.
Thou hath saved Freedom's Spirit
Of my Stormy Youth, the idol
Forgotten by Society's gossiping discourse.
Far from Neva's shores
Before me Caucasia's proud heads
Are spread
Above their summits steep,
Above the rocky slopes deep.
I am nourished with sombre dreams,
With fascinating scenes
Of a land wonderfully wild and grim.
But the same oppressive dream
As before, my soul ever doth inspire
Long in me is extinguished Poetry's fire.
In vain am I seeking here impressions.
It hath vanished from me my age of passion.
O love and the inspira tions of the heart,
The days of rapture forever did depart
From me; and from me too is hidden long
The goddess of peaceful song.

1817–1820

TALE OF TSAR SALTAN,

OF HIS SON THE FAMOUS AND PUISSANT CHAMPION GVIDON SALTANOVICH, AND OF THE LOVELY SWAN-PRINCESS

TALE OF TSAR SALTAN

By their window sat and spun
Maidens three; the day was done.
And the eldest maid was saying:
"Were I empress, I'd be laying
Out in state a banquet fine,
For the whole wide world to dine."
And the second maid was saying:
"Were I empress, I'd be laying
Linen out, and weave by hand,
For the whole world, every strand."
Then the youngest spoke, the other:
"Were I empress, I'd be mother
Of a hero; I would bear
To our father-tsar an heir."

Scarce that maid had ended speaking,
When the door went softly creaking,
And the emperor stept inside,
Lord of all that country wide.
All the while they were debating,
He behind the fence was waiting,
And the youngest sister's word
Pleased him best of all he heard.
"Beauteous maiden, happy meeting!
Be my empress! Such his greeting.
"Bear me that same hero son
Ere September's out and done.
You, beloved sisters, quitting
This poor chamber, must be flitting

In my train, and follow now—
Follow, too, your sister. Thou
Shalt be cook, and thou, the second,
Lady-webster shalt be reckoned."

Father-tsar went in the hall;
To the palace hastened all.
Tsar Saltan, not long he tarried;
On that evening he was married.
Noble was the feast; thereat
With his youthful queen he sat.
Then the noble guests attended
To a couch of ivory splendid
Bride and bridegroom, young and fair,
And alone they left them there.

Sent a rider with a scroll
To rejoice the father's soul.
But, to compass her undoing,
Cook and webster plots were brewing
To forestall that messenger;
Babarikha, dowager,
Grandam, aiding; and another
Was dispatched, with this: "The mother
Yesternight gave birth to one
Neither frog, nor mouse, nor son—
No, nor daughter; but a creature
Monstrous, new, and out of nature."

When the rider brought that word,
And tsar, the father, heard,

Cook, within the kitchen railing,
Webster at the loom bewailing,
Grudge the good things that befall
Such a spouse imperial.
But the lady, young and royal,
To the word she gave was loyal,
And that night became with child.

These were times of war, and wild.
Tsar Saltan, on point of parting,
On his trusty charger starting,
Bade his queen: "From every ill
Keep thyself, and love me still."
While he far away was faring
Long, and pitilessly warring,
Came her time at last; and God
Brought a boy—of too foot odd.
With her babe the empress resting,
Like a mother-eagle nesting,

First he bade him hang, in passion;
Bore himself in strangest fashion,
Yet, for once relenting, gave
These commands unto the slave:
"Wait: the emperor, returning,
Shall adjudge, by law and learning."

With the writing forth he passed,
Rode, and got him home at last.
Cook and webster and that other,
Babarikha, the queen-mother,
Gave the word to ply him deep,
Got him in drunken sleep,
Robbed his wallet of the writing,
Planted one of their inditing.
So that day the fuddled man
Brought the order; thus it ran:
"These, to our boyars: Obey ye.
Not an idle hour delay ye.

Queen and brood fling privily
In the bottomless deep sea."
And the good boyars, they failed not;
Nought would serve;
and grief availed not
For their lord and mistress young.
So into her room they flung,
Told how both must meet disaster
At the bidding of the master;
Read the order out; anon
Set the empress and her son
In a barrel; and the thickly,
Tarred it over, rolled it quickly,
Drove it duly forth to sea.
"Thus he told us; thus do we."

In the dry land wash and lay us!"
There and then the obedient wave
Gently to the foreshore drave
Freight and barrel; left them stranded;
Noiseless ebbed; behold them landed!
Child and queen are safe ashore,
And she feels the earth once more.
—Who from out the cask shall take them?
Surely God will not forsake them?
On his feet the boy stands straight,
At the bottom drives his pate,
Gives a little heave, and asks then,
"How are windows cut in casks, then,
For escape?—without ado
Bursts the bottom, and comes through.

In the blue sky stars are flashing;
On the blue sea waves are lashing;
Stormy cloud the sky bedims;
On the sea the barrel swims.
There the queen lies, struggling, straining,
Like a woeful widow plaining.
Every hour the child hath grown
Fast as though a day were flown.
Still she wails; and still he urges,
As the day goes by, the surges:—
"Wave, my wave, beloved of me!
Thou art boisterous and free;
Wheresoe'er thou wilt thou splashest,
Shingle upon shingle dashest,
Flooding all the shores that be,
Hoisting vessels on the sea.
I command three, do not slay us;

Now the pair are free to wander.
See, a champaign rises yonder
To a hill with green oaks crowned,
With the blue sea spanning round.
But the son and heir was heedful,
Holding a good supper needful;
Snapped an oaken branch, and so
Bent it in a stubborn bow;
From his cross* a silk cord taking,
Strung it on the bow, and breaking
Short a slender reed, made right
A good arrow, sharp and light.
Then he went for quarry forward
To the valley-edges shoreward.

To the beach he scarce had gone,
When he heard—was that a moan?—

* The cross which every Orthodox wears around his neck from a child.

БАЖЕНОВ. П. С. ПАЛЕХ. 1934 г.

Saw the sea disturbed,—and, gazing,
Something evil and amazing:—
In the wave, a swan shows fight,
And above her hangs a kite.
And the poor bird wildly splashes,
And the troubled water lashes;
He his needle-claws outflings,
Whets his gory neb;—then sings
All at once the arrow speeding,
Strikes his crop, and sends him bleeding
Out his life into the flow.
And the prince, with lowered bow,
Sees the creature sink and flutter
With a cry no bird could utter.
And the swan floats round, and still
Pecks that kite of wicked will,
Batters him with wing descending,
Drowns him, for a quicker ending.
Then to the tsarevich young
Speaks she in the Russian tongue:
"Thou, my prince, wert my salvation,
Mighty for my liberation.
Grieve not that because of me
Thy good shaft lies under sea,
Or that thou must fast to-morrow:
Sorrow proves not always sorrow.

Richly shalt thou be repaid,
And hereafter have my aid.
Saviour of a swan thou seemest,
But a maid to life redeemest;
With thy arrow thou didst smite
An enchanter, and no kite.
Know, that always I shall mind thee;
Be thou where thou mayst, I find thee.
Now, however, homeward get.
Go; sleep sound; no longer fret."

So flew off swan enchanted.
Queen and prince held firm, and scanted,
Though a livelong day had passed;
Bedward went, nor broke their fast.
Next the prince, his eyes unclosing,
Shook away his dreams and dozing,
And behold! To his amaze,
A great city met his gaze.
White the walls were, and behind them
Thick the battlements that lined them;
Church and sacred cloister there
Sparkle, turreted in air.
Quick the queen is roused and sighing
Oh! and *ah*! The prince is crying
"Will the thing come true? I see,

Pleasant is my swan with me."
To the city both betake them,
Cross the barrier; to make them
Welcome, triply surge and swell
Deafening chimes from every bell.
And the folk flood out to meet them;
Holy choirs praise God, and greet them;
In gold chariots to the gate
Comes the court in princely state.
All men praise and honour loudly
That tsarevich; crown him proudly
With a prince's cap; declare
He is monarch of all there.
License of the queen obtaining,
On that day the prince is reigning

Whither may ye now be ranging?"
Then the sailor-men speak out:
"We have sailed the world about:
Now in sables we have traded,
Now in foxes dusky-shaded.
Past the island of Buyan,
To the realm of famed Saltan
Now due eastward we are wending.
Time is up; our trip is ending."
"Happy journey, every man,
To the famous tsar Saltan
Over sea and ocean faring!"
So the prince gave word, declaring:
"Do him reverence from me!"
Then they went, and, gazing, he

In his capital; thereon
Takes the name of *Prince Gvidon*
Breezes on the water shifting
Landward urge a vessel drifting,
Bellying out her canvas brave
As she skims along the wave.
On the deck the shipmen teeming
Wonder if awake or dreaming
Such a marvel they behold
On that island, known of old—
Strongly gated quays, and gilded
Towers; a city newly builded!
Cannon flaming from the quay
Bid the ship put in from sea;
And the strangers by the gateway
Moor; the prince invites them straightway,
Gives them food and drink, and then
Thus makes question of the men:
"Merchants, what are ye exchanging?

Watched them far, beheld them vanish,
Sad with thoughts he might not banish.
Look! The snowy swan, aswim
On the billows, calls to him
"Hail, my lovely prince, good morrow!
Tell me, tell me, my prince, thy sorrow?
Why art thou so silent, say,
Downcast as a rainy day?"
"I've a weary grief devouring,
All my manhood overpowering.
Would I might my father see!"
Dolefully thus answered he.
But the swan said, "Art thou minded
To pursue the ship? behind it
Flit, and be a midget, since
This is all thy woe, my prince!"
Then she waved her wings, and scattered
Noisily the wave, and spattered
Him with spray from top to toe.

In a single instant, lo,
To a dot he shrank and minished,
Was a midge; the change was finished.
Piping soft, away flew he,
Caught the vessel on the sea,
Lighted gently, to discover
A good cranny, and took cover.

Past the island of Buyan,
To the realm of famed Saltan
Gaily onward flies the trader,
Gaily hums the breeze to aid her;
See, already looming nigher
Is the land of her desire!
Soon the strangers, newly landed,
To the palace are commanded,
And behind them to the king
Our adventurer takes wing.
There he sees, in gold all shining,
But with countenance repining,
Crowned and throned above them all,
King Saltan within his hall.
Cook and webster and that other,
Babarikha the queen-mother,
Pin their looks upon the king,
Squatting round him in a ring.
Then he calls the guests and seats them:
At his board; with question greets them:
"Master-merchants, where go ye?
Sailed ye long? and over sea
Fared ye well? Or lived ye poorly?
In the world are wonders, surely?"
Then the sailor-men speak out:
"We have sailed the world about.
Overseas we lived not poorly;
Here was a world's wonder, surely?—
Once an island in the deep
Lay unpeopled, barren, steep,
Blank and level; on it growing
Was a single oak-tree showing.
There to-day a city new
With a palace stands to view.
Golden-steepled churches cap it,
Towers ascend, and gardens lap it,
There sits prince Gvidon, and thence
Sends to thee his reverence."
At the tale astonished duly,
"If I live," the tsar said, "truly
I will see that wondrous isle,

Have Gvidon my host awhile."
Cook and webster and the other,
Babarikha, the queen-mother,
All were loth to let him so
To that isle of wonders go.
Said the cook, malignly winking
To her fellows, "We are thinking
That a city by the sea
Surely is a prodigy!
Hear, now, of no paltry wonder:—
In a wood a pine, whereunder
Sings a squirrel rhyme on rhyme,
Nibbling filberts all the time:
Common filberts they are not, sir;
Each a golden shell has got, sir;
Kernels, of pure emerald:
Which a wonder may be called."
Tsar Saltan sat there, astounded;
But the midge, in wrath unbounded,

At his auntie drove his sting,
In her right eye plunged the thing.
And cook went pale, and wried her
Visage, swooning; and beside her
Slave and sister, mother too,
With a shriek the midge pursue.
"Insect double-damned!" they fidget,
"We will show thee...!" but the midget
Calmly through the casement flees
To his home beyond the seas.

Prince again, the shore he paces;
Still the azure sea he faces.
Look! the snowy swan, aswim
On the billows, calls to him:
"Hail, my lovely prince, good morrow!
Tell me, tell me, prince, thy sorrow?
Why art thou so silent, say,
Downcast as a rainy day?"
Then he answers, "Ay, a dreary
Grief consumes me; I am weary
To discover, if I could,
One great marvel:—in a wood
Somewhere stands a pine, whereunder
(Hark you, 'tis no paltry wonder)
Chants a squirrel rhyme on rhyme,
Nibbling filberts all the time:
Common filberts they are, not, ma'am;
Kernels of pure emerald, too!
Ah, the tale may not be true!"
But the swan replies, "No fable
Is that squirrel; I am able
Of this marvel to make sure.
Prince, dear heart, lament no more;
Hold; for I with joy will lend thee
Any service, to befriend thee."

So with heart uplifted high
Home he goes, and drawing nigh
The wide courtyard, lo! is gazing
On a fir of height amazing
Where a squirrel, before all,

Gnaws the golden nuts that fall,
Out of each an emerald shelling,
And the empty husks is telling
Into many an even pile,
Chanting, whistling all the while
To those noble folk a ditty:
Is it in the garden pretty,
Or the kitchen-plot? Gvidon,
Wondering sorely, thanks the swan:
"Lord, bestow on her such blessing
Even as I am now possessing!"
For the squirrel then he bade
That a crystal house be made;
Set a clerk to make an entry
Strict, of every nut; a sentry
Also at the doorway pitched.
—Squirrel honoured, prince enriched!

Breezes on the water shifting
Landward urge a vessel drifting,

Raising up her canvas brave
As she skims along the wave
Past the island cliff-defended,
Past the city large and splendid.
Cannon flaming from the quay
Bid the ship put in from sea.
Then the merchants by the gateway
Moor; the prince invites them straightway,
Gives them food and drink, and then
Thus makes question of the men:
"Merchants, what are ye exchanging?
Whither may ye now be ranging?"
And the sailor-men speak out:
"We have sailed the world about;
All the while in the horses trading,
Stallions from the Don our lading.
Past the island of Buyan
To the realm of famed Saltan
Far the path that we are wending.
Time is up; our trip is ending."
"Happy journey, every man,
To the famous tsar Saltan
Over sea and ocean faring!"
So the prince gave word, declaring
"Homage take from Prince Gvidon
To the tsar upon his throne."

Then the merchants bowed, departed,
Straight upon their voyage started.
Seaward stept the prince; thereon
Through the waters rode the swan.
"Ah," he prayed, "my soul is longing,
Swept away by wishes thronging..."
In a moment, as before,
She besprinkled him all o'er,
And the prince became a fly then,
And between the sea and sky then
Winged away, and on the ship
Lighted, in a chink to slip.

Past the island of Buyan
To the realm of famed Saltan
Gaily onward flies the trader,
Gaily hums the breeze to aid her.
See, already looming nigher
Is the land of her desire!
Soon the merchants, newly landed,
To the palace are commanded,
And behind them to the king
Our adventurer takes wing.
There he sees, in gold all shining,
But with countenance repining,
Crowned and throned above them all
Tsar Saltan within his hall.
Webster; wry-faced cook; that other,
Babarikha the queen-mother,—
Glower like toads upon the king,
Squatting round him in a ring.
Then he calls the merchants, seats them
At his board, with question greets them:
"Strangers, masters, where go ye?
Sailed ye long? and on the sea
Fared ye well? Or lived ye poorly?
In the world are wonders, surely?"
Then the sailor-men speak out:
"We have sailed the world about;
Overseas we lived not poorly;
Here was a world's wonder, surely—
On the deep an island lies;
There we saw a city rise;

Golden-steepled churches cap it,
Towers ascend, and gardens lap it.
By a palace is a fir
And a house of crystal, sir;
There a squirrel tame is thriving
And what tricks is she contriving!
She is chanting rhyme on rhyme,
Nibbling filberts all the time—
Common filberts they are not, sir!
Each a golden shell has got, sir!
Kernels, too, of emerald pure.
Guarded there, she sits secure;
Henchmen sundry service tender,
And a clerk is set to render
Count of every nut; at hand
Doing honour, soldiers stand,
Cast those shell in coin, and send them
Round, for all the world to spend them.
Maidens too the emeralds strow
Into padlockt stores below
All are rich men in that islet,
Nobly housed; no huts defile it.
There sits Prince Gvidon, and thence
Sends to thee his reverence."
At the tale astonished duly,
"If I live," the tsar said, "truly
I will see the wondrous isle,
Have Gvidon my host awhile."
Cook and webster and that other,
Babarikha the queen-mother,
All are loth to let him so
To that isle of wonders go.
And the webster with a lurking
Snigger to tsar said, smirking:
"Was it wondrous, what they saw?
Did a squirrel pebbles gnaw,
Gold about at random shaking,
Emeralds in bunches raking?
Be it lies or be it truth,
We are not amazed, in sooth.
For the world a greater wonder
Holds:—a sea that swells in thunder,
Boils tempestuously o'er,
Floods on a deserted shore,

Sunders, noisily careering.
See, upon that shore appearing,
Blazing fierily, there be
Scale-clad champions, thirty-three!
Each is comely, each defiant,
Each a pickt and youthful giant;
All of even height; one more
Follows—uncle Chernomor.
Say now, is not this thing rarely
Wonderful, to call in fairly?"
And the guests, who have the wit
Not to cross her, silent sit.
Tsar Saltan is sore astounded;
But Gvidon, in wrath unbounded;
In a flash, a buzzing fly,
Lights on auntie's leftward eye;
And that webster paled, to find it
Instantly and wholly blinded.
"Catch him, catch him," still they yell;
"Squash him, squash him, squash him well!
Now we have him; stay, keep still there!"
—Calmly, past the window-sill there,
To his heritage now flees
Prince Gvidon, beyond the seas.

By the shore the prince is pacing,
Ever on the blue sea facing;
Look! the snowy swan, aswim
On the billows, calls to him:
"Hail, my lovely prince, good morrow!
Tell me, tell me, whence thy sorrow?
Why art thou so silent, say,
Downcast as a rainy day?"
Then he answers, "Ay, a dreary
Grief consumes me; I am weary
For a marvel; would there were
Such a windfall, for my share!"
"Tell me, what might be that wonder?"
"Somewhere, ocean, swells in thunder,
Boils tempestuously o'er,
Floods on a deserted shore,
Spills, in noisy spray careering.

And upon that, shore appearing,
Blazing fierily, there be
Scale-clad champions, thirty-three.
Each is comely, each defiant,
Each a pickt and youthful giant,
All of even height; one more
Follows—uncle Chernomor."
"Here is nothing to disquiet;
Dear one, be not troubled by it,"
So the swan replies; "for well
Know I that same miracle.
Why, those knights, whom ocean mothers,
Are my true-begotten brothers.
Grieve not; go; the brethren wait;
Give them welcome at thy gate."

Then he sat, no longer troubled,
In his tower; the waters bubbled;
On the sea his eyes he turned;
Suddenly the ocean churned,
Loudly splashed, and fled, and parted.
On the foreshore up there started
Each one blazing fierily,
Scale-clad champions thirty-three.
Two and two they march; conveying
Citywards the troop, with graying
Locks that glitter, Chernomor,
That good uncle, goes before.
From his tower the prince came posting,
Those dear visitors accosting.

Swiftly scurried up the folk;
To the prince the uncle spoke:
"Bidden by the swan, we landed;
Straitly she hath us commanded
That we guard thy glorious town
And patrol it, up and down.
We are daily now to sally
From the ocean wave, and rally,
Never failing, one and all,
By thy lofty city wall.
Soon we meet again; now leave us;
We must forth to sea, for grievous
Unto us is earthly air."
One and all, they homeward fare.

Breezes on the water shifting
Landward urge a vessel drifting,
Raising up her canvas brave
As she skims along the wave
Past the island cliff-defended,
Past the city large and splendid.
Cannon flaming from the quay
Bid the ship put in from sea.
Then the merchants by the gateway
Moor; the prince invites them straightway;
Gives them food and drink, and then
Thus makes question of the men:
"Merchants, what are ye exchanging?
Whither may ye now be ranging?"
And the sailor-men speak out:
"We have sailed the world about;
Virgin silver, gold, and bladed
Steel are wares that we have traded.
Past the island of Buyan
To the realm of famed Saltan
Far the path that we are wending.
Time is up; our trip is ending."
"Happy journey, every man,
To the famous tsar Saltan
Over sea and ocean faring!"
So the prince gave word, declaring
"Homage take from prince Gvidon
To the tsar upon his throne."

Then the merchants bowed, departed,
Straight upon their voyage started.
Seaward stept the prince; thereon
Through the waters rode the swan.
"Ah," he cried, "My soul is longing,
Swept away by wishes thronging..."
In a moment, as before,
She besprinkled him all o'er;
There and then he shrank and minished
To a humble-bee; 'twas finished;
Flying, droning, off went he,
Caught the vessel on the sea,
Lighted softly, to discover
Aft a cranny, and took cover.

Past the island of Buyan,
To the realm of famed Saltan
Gaily onward runs the trader,
Gaily hums the breeze to aid her.
See, already looming nigher
Is the land of her desire!
Soon the merchants newly landed
To the palace are commanded,
And behind them to the king
Our adventurer takes wing.
There he sees, in gold all shining,
But with countenance repining,
Crowned and throned above them all
Tsar Saltan within his hall.

Cook, and webster, and that other,
Babarikha, the queen-mother,
All the trio, in a ring,
Gaze, foursquare, upon the king.
Then he calls the merchants, seat them
At his board, with question greets them:
"Merchants, masters, where go ye?
Sailed ye long, and on the sea
Fared ye well? or lived ye poorly?
In the world are wonders, surely?"
Then the sailor-men speak out:
"We have sailed the world about;
Overseas we lived not poorly;
Here was a world's wonder, surely:—
On the deep an island lies;
There a city doth arise;
And each day there comes a wonder:
For the ocean swells in thunder,
Boils tempestuously o'er,
Floods on a deserted shore,
Spills, in noisy spray careering.
Then upon that shore appearing,
Blazing fierily, there be
Scale-clad champions thirty-three.
Each is comely, each defiant,
Each a pickt and youthful giant;
All of even height; one more,
Ancient uncle Chernomor,
With them from the ocean sallies,
And in twos the troop he rallies
To protect that island-town
And patrol it up and down.
Never was a guard securer,
Braver, busier, or surer.
There sits Prince Gvidon,
and thence
Sends to thee his reverence."

At the tale astonished duly,
"If I live," the tsar said, "truly
To that wondrous isle I'll come,
Guest of Prince Gvidon." But mum
Cook and webster sit; that other,
Babarikha, the queen-mother,
Snickering cries, "Shall sailor-men
With this tale amaze us, then?
People out of ocean strolling
Wander prowling and patrolling!
Whether lies or truth they tell,
Here I see no miracle.
Can such marvels be? a new one
I will tell ye, and a true one:—
Over sea a princess stays;
None from her can take his gaze;
She bedims the sun in heaven;
She illumes the earth at even;
Moonbeams in her tresses are;
On her forehead burns a star;
And herself, she sails before ye
Like a peafowl in her glory;
When she speaks, her accent seem
Like the warble of a stream.
Say now, is not this thing rarely
Wonderful, to call it fairly?"
And the guests, who have the wit
Not to cross her, silent sit.
Tsar Saltan is sore astounded;
But the prince, his wrath unbounded

Reining, at his grandma flies,
But he spares her ancient eyes.
Round he twirls, and drones, and flounces,
Straight upon her nose he pounces,
And that nose the hero strings;
Up a mighty blister springs;
Then once more alarm is sounded:
"Help—in Heaven's name—confound it!—
Catch him, catch him!" now they yell,
Squash him, squash him, squash him well!
Now we have him—stay, be still there!"
But the humble clears the sill there;
To his heritage he flees,
Calmly flitting overseas.

By the shore the prince is pacing,
Ever on the blue sea facing.
Look! the snowy swan, aswim
On the billows, call to him:
"Hail, my lovely prince, good morrow!
Tell me, tell me, whence thy sorrow?
Why art thou so silent, say,
Downcast as a rainy day?"
"I am wretched, and a dreary
Grief consumes me; I am weary
Watching other people wed,
All but me—", he sadly said.
"But who is she? by what token
Shalt thou know her? "Men have spoken
Of a princess. Where she dwells,
The beholder sees nought else.
She bedims the sun in heaven;
She illumes the earth at even;

Moonbeams in her tresses are;
On her forehead burns a star;
And herself, she walks before ye
Like a peafowl in her glory;
When she speaks, her accent seem
Like the warble of a stream.
Only—is this truth or error?"
He awaits her word, in terror.
Silently the snowy swan
Mused awhile, but spoke anon:
"Such a maid there is; but take her
Once to wife, thou canst not shake her
Like a mitten from thy wrist;
No, nor like a girdle twist.
Hear my counsel; thou shalt profit,
So thou wilt avail thee of it:
Ponder all things; hesitate,
Lest repentance come, too late."
But he swore he would not tarry;
Time was ripe for him to marry;
He had turned it every way
In his thoughts; was ready, nay,
Passionately yearned to wander
After that fair princess yonder;
Fain to trudge it, if need be,
To the world's extremity.
Then the swan—profoundly
signed she—
"Why so far afield, replied she,
"For thy princess? I am she;
Here behold thy destiny."

Then, her pinions upward flinging,
Over the wide water swinging,
Down she stooped upon the strand,
Hid her in a bush at hand,
Gave a shake and gave a shiver,
Turned a princess, with one quiver.
Moonbeams in her tresses are;
On her forehead burns a star;
And the lady, in her glory
Like a peafowl walks before ye;

№ 2856 п Палех
Е. Небогатова

When she speaks, her accent seem
Like the warble of a stream.
Then and there the prince enfolds her
To his bosom white, and holds her;
Then to his dear mother he
Leads her quickly; on his knee
Falls, and thus begins entreating!
"Sovereign lady-mother, greeting!
This my chosen bride shall be
Duteous daughter unto thee.
Grant this boon, that we, possessing
Thy good leave and marriage-blessing,
May in peace and concord live;
So, thy benediction give."
Then the ikon she extended
Wonder-working, o'er their bended
Heads, and wept, and spoke:
"The Lord
You, my children, shall reward."
But the prince, not long he tarried,
To the princess he was married,
And they entered on their life,
Waiting increase, man and wife.

Breezes on the water shifting
Landward urge a vessel drifting,
Bellying out her canvas brave
As she skims along the wave
Past the island cliff-defended,
Past the city large and splendid.
Cannon flaming from the quay
Bid the ship put in from sea;
And the merchants by the gateway
Moor; the prince invites them straightway,
Gives them food and drink, and then
Thus makes question of the men:
"Merchants, what are ye exchanging?
Whither may ye now be ranging?"
And the sailor-men speak out:
"We have sailed the world about;
Contraband has been our lading.
Past the island of Buyan

To the realm of famed Saltan
On a far road we are wending,
Eastward, home; our trip is ending."
"Happy journey, every man,
To the famous tsar Saltan
Over sea and ocean faring!"
So the prince gave word, declaring,
"Mark, your sovereign made a vow
He would be my guest; till now
Never has he stirred; remind him.
Of that promise, when ye find him.
Take him homage, too, from me."
So they went their ways; but he
This time stayed at home, nor started;
Would not from his wife be parted.

Past the island of Buyan,
To the realm of famed Saltan
Gaily onward runs the trader,
Gaily hums the breeze to aid her.
Now the old familiar shore
Looms in sight for them once more,
And the strangers, newly landed,
To the palace are commanded,
And the emperor they behold
Sitting there and crowned with gold.
Cook, and webster, and that other,
Babarikha, the queen-mother,
All the trio, in a ring,
Gaze, foursquare, upon the king.
Then he calls the merchants, seats them
At his board, with questions greets them:
"Merchants, masters, where go ye?
Sailed ye long? and on the sea
Fared ye well? or lived ye poorly?
In the world are wonders, surely?"
Then the sailor-men speak out:
"We have sailed the world about;
Overseas we lived not poorly;
Here was a world's wonder, surely:—
On the deep an island lies;
There a city doth arise;

Golden-steepled churches cap it;
Towers ascend, and gardens lap it.
By the palace is a pine,
And a mansion crystalline;
There a squirrel tame is thriving;
And such tricks is she contriving!
She is chanting rhyme on rhyme,
Nibbling filberts all the time;
Common filberts they are not, sir;
Kernels too, of emerald pure;
Each a golden shell has got, sir!
Her they pet, and keep secure.

And there is a further wonder:
There the ocean swells in thunder,
Boils tempestuously o'er,
Floods on the deserted shore,
Spills, in noisy spray careering;
And upon that shore appearing,
Blazing fierily, there be
Scale-clad champions, thirty-three.
Each is comely, each defiant,
Each a pickt and youthful giant,
All of even height; one more
Follows, uncle Chernomor.
Never was a guard securer,
Braver, busier, or surer.
With the prince a bride there stays;
None from her can take his gaze;
She bedims the sun in heaven;
She illumes the earth at even;
Moonbeams in her tresses are;
On her forehead burns a star.
Prince Gvidon that city proudly
Rules, and all men praise him loudly.
And he sends thee homage now,
Yet he blames thee: "Where's thy vow
Soon to be our guest, nor linger;
Yet thou never stirrest finger!"

Then the tsar could not forbear
Longer; bade the fleet prepare.
Cook, and webster, and that other,
Babarikha the queen-mother,
All were loth to let him so
To that isle of wonders go.
But the monarch, nothing heeding,
Silenced then and there their pleading,
Saying, "Is Saltan a child
Or tsar?", and never smiled;
Stampt, and cried, "I sail this morning!"
Left them; slammed the door,
in warning.

Prince Gvidon, all silently
At his window watched the sea;
Not a murmur, or a lashing
Wave, but just a gentle plashing!
But upon the distance blue
Ships were swimming into view:
"Twas the emperor's fleet in motion
Coming o'er the level ocean.
Then the prince Gvidon upsprang,
Thunderous his summons rang:
"Mother of my heart, come hither!
Thou too, young princess; and thither
Turn your eyes, upon the sea;
"This my father comes to me."

And he sees the fleet draw nearer;
Points a spyglass, marks it clearer;
Sees on deck the emperor pass
Spying at them through his glass.
Cook and webster and the other,
Babarikha the queen-mother
By his side bewildered stand
At that unfamiliar land.
Guns flame out from every barrel,
Every belfry chimes a carol.
Prince Gvidon goes down, and he
Meets the tsar beside the sea,
Cook and webster and that other,
Babarikha the queen-mother.
Quickly he the tsar has brought
To the city, saying nought.

To the palace all go straightway.
Armour gleams beside the gateway.
There the emperor can see
Thirty champions and three.
Each is comely, each defiant,
Each a pickt and youthful giant;
All one stature; and one more
Follows, uncle Chernomor.
Next, the tsar the court is treading,
Where, beneath a pine high-spreading
Chants a squirrel rhyme on rhyme,
Nibbling gold nuts all the time,
Out of each an emerald cropping,
In a sack the jewel dropping;
And the spacious court is strewn
With the golden husks alone.
Further still— on what amazing
Princess are the strangers gazing?
Moonbeams in her tresses are;
On her forehead burns a star,
And herself she walks before ye
Like a peafowl in her glory,
And her prince's mother leads.
And the tsar, he gazes, heeds,
Knows them both; his heart is leaping;
"What is here? he cried, and weeping
Melted, and his breath he drew
Hard and heavily, and knew
Her, his queen, and quickly caught her
To him, and his gallant daughter
And his son. To board they fared
And a noble banquet shared.
Cook and webster and that other,
Babarikha the queen-mother,
Into corners scampered round;
Hardly might those three be found.
Then they broke in sobs and moaning,
All their past transgressions owning,
And the tsar, so glad was he,
Merely banished home the three.
And they bore to bed, half-drunken,
Tsar Saltan, when day was sunken.

I drank beer, drank mead; and yet
Hardly were my whiskers wet.

1831

и. Голиков 1933г.

Вот мудрец перед Дадоном
Стал и вынул из мешка
Золотого петушка.
А. ВАТАГИН
ПАЛЕХ

THE GOLDEN COCK

THE GOLDEN COCK

Once—in Kingdom Twenty-Seven
Or the Realm of Thrice Eleven—
Somewhere—reigned a tsar, Dodon,
Terrible and famous, known
From his youth for rashly wronging
All his neighbours. He was longing,
Now that age was creeping close,
To make sure of his repose
And relax from wars and labours.
Now behold, those very neighbours
Harried him, with damage sore
To that aged emperor.

So, to hinder them from raiding
On his frontiers, and invading,
He must needs maintain a host,
Multitudes at every post.
Sleepless, still his captains waited;
Vainly!—they are still belated.
Are they watching southward? no,
From the east comes down the foe.
That amended—see, from ocean
Those untoward guests in motion!
Tsar Dodon can only weep
Tears of rage, and lose his sleep.

What is life, in such conditions
Of disquiet? He petitions
Next for aid an eunuch sage,
Both astrologer and mage.
Couriers fly, and make obeisance;
Soon the wise man is in presence
Of Dodon; and from his poke
Out he pulls a Golden Cock,
Saying, "Take this fowl, and set him
On a perch aloft; and let him,
This my Golden Cockerel,
Be your trusty sentinel.
He, when all is peace about you,
Shall sit still; but never doubt you
That the moment from afar
Comes the least surmise of war
Or incursion, to beset you,
Mischief unforeknown, to threat you,
Then my Cockerel instantly
Shall perk up his comb on high
Veering towards the danger, shuffling,
Crowing, and his feathers ruffling."
Then his thanks the emperor told
To the eunuch; piles of gold
Proffered, rapt in admiration;
Cried, "For such an obligation,
Shall the earliest wish of thine
Be fulfilled, as though 'twere mine!"

So the Cock became the warder,
Perched on high, of every border.
If that faithful watcher e'er
Noted peril anywhere,
He, as though from sleep awaking,
Veered towards it, shuffling, shaking;
And "*Kiri-ku-ku!*" he said;
"Rule them, as you lie abed!"
And those neighbours soon were quiet,
Had no heart for war or riot,
When the tsar on every hand
Made so resolute a stand.
This year flies, and then another.
Cock sits quiet, makes no pother.
But one day a monstrous noise
Tsar Dodon's repose destroys.
"Father of thy people! master!
Rouse thee, sire! Behold disaster!"
Thus aloud the captain cries.
Through his yawns the tsar replies:
"Eh, who's there? what is it, say you,
Sirs? and *what* disaster, pray you?"
Says the captain, "Noise and fear
Fill thy capital; we hear
Once again the Cockerel crowing."
And the emperor, quickly going
To his window, sees the beast
Flapping, turning to the east.

"Not the time to loiter! hurry,
All to horse! and all men, scurry!"
Off his elder son is sent
Eastward, with an armament.
Then the Cock gives over flapping.
All is peace. The tsar lies napping.
Eight days pass; but not a word
Of that army has been heard.
Has it fought, or not? No message
Comes unto Dodon. In presage
Yet again Cockerel crows
Out a second muster goes,
And the tsar sends forth the other
Son, to aid his elder brother.
Silent is the Cock once more.
Still no tidings; as before,
Eight days pass; and all the nation
Lives them through in consternation.
Now again the crow is heard!
And the tsar conducts a third
Muster eastward, never knowing
What may be the good of going.
Night and day those troops marched on
Till their strength was all but gone;
And the emperor, never sighting
Any camp, or field of fighting,
Or sepulchral barrow, thought,
"How is such a wonder wrought?"
Even with the eighth day's ending
With his host he was ascending
Lofty mountains. In their heart
Stood a silken tent apart
With a magic silence round it.
Near, an army lay; he found it
In a narrow gorge, all dead.
To the tent the monarch sped,
There a dreadful scene descrying:
Both his sons before him lying
Lifeless, mail and helmet gone,
And the weapon of each one
Through the other's body. Yonder
In the mead their horses wander
On the trampled turf, and pass
Through the blood-besprinkled grass.
Then the tsar, with anguish shaken,
Moaned, "Ah, woe! my children taken,
Both our falcons snared! and I—
It is time for me to die."

And they all took up his moaning,
And a slow and heavy groaning
Pierced the vales, and quivers went
Through the hills. But swift the tent
Parted wide; and thence, all splendid
As the dawn, a maid descended
—Queen of Shamakhan was she—
Softly to the tsar; and he,
Mute, like owl by sunshine blinded,
Gazed into her eyes, nor minded
In her presence both his sons
Lying dead. But she at once
Smiled on tsar Dodon, and to him
Curtseyed deep, and took
and drew him
By the hand, and made him go
Into her own tent; and so
To a table next she led him,
And on many dainties fed him;
Bade him rest, and saw him laid
On a bed of rich brocade.
There, for just a week, beglamoured
And enchanted and enamoured,
Tsar Dodon with her made feast,
Her obedient slave and guest.
Now at last Dodon is speeding
Back, his valiant army leading;
Turns his steps to home again,
With the lady in his train.
Rumour runs before him, crying
Sometimes truth, and often lying.
Near the city gates the throng
By the chariot rush along,
Noisily the empress meeting
And the tsar, who gives his greeting
Unto all; but quickly he
In the crowd a head doth see
Grey as any swan's, and on it
Is a Saracen white bonnet.
'Tis the eunuch, his old friend!

"Ha, good father! heaven send
Health to thee; how now, come nigher;
Tell us, what is thy desire!"
Said the wise man: "Now at last,
Tsar, our long account we cast.
Mind'st thou, for my service, making
Once a friendly undertaking
That the earliest wish of mine
Should be granted, as 'twere thine?
Queen of Shamakhan."
In the wonder
Stood the tsar, and thus spoke he:
"Ancient, what hath taken thee?
Some possession of the devil?
Hast thou lost thy wits? what evil
Fancy entered thy head?
There are bounds, when all is said,
Though I made the promise duly.
What to thee are maidens, truly?
Peace, enough. For dost thou know
Who I am? I will bestow
Title of boyar, or treasure,
Or a war-horse, at thy pleasure,
From our stables. Thou canst have
Half my kingdom."
"Nought I crave;
Give me nothing but lady,
Queen of Shamakhan." So prayed he;
Ever thus the sage replied.
But the tsar, he spat, and cried,
"What, so bold? then nought thou gainest,
Sinner! thus thyself thou painest;
Go, with bones unbroken still;
Drag him hence! It is my will."
Then the old man fell to wrangling;
But, with certain people, jangling
Pays not; for the sceptre now
Caught him just upon the brow.
Flat he fell, and life departed.
All the city shuddered, started.

Cried the maid, "Ho ho! He he!
Here's a fearless sinner, see!"
And, though sore perturbed, a tender
Smile the tsar contrived to send her.
Then he rode within the town.
  But there came a rustle down,
And the city stared affrighted;
For the Cock flew forth, alighted,
Winging straightway to the car,
On the skull of that great tsar;
Flapped, and gave one peck, and flitted
Upward; and, as earth he quitted,
From the chariot dropt Dodon,
Dying with a single groan.
  And, as thought that queen had never
Lived, she vanished, and for ever.
  Though my story is not true,
'Tis a lesson, lads, to you.

1834

№ 1184

С. Палех И. Баканов 1934 г.

TALE OF THE POPE AND OF HIS WORK-MAN BALDA

Porridge-head
was a pope, who is dead.
He went out a-shopping one day
To look for some wares on the way;
And he came on Baldà, who was there,
Who was going he knew not where,
And who said, "Why so early abroad, old sire?
And what dost require?"
He replied, "For a workman I look,
To be stableman, carpenter, cook;
But where to procure
Such a servant?—a cheap one, be sure!"
Says Baldà, "I will come as thy servant,
I'll be splendid, and punctual, and fervent;
And my pay for the year is—three raps on the head;
Only, give me boiled wheat when I'm fed."
Then he pondered, that pope;
Scratched his poll, put his hope
In his luck, in the Russian *Perhaps*.
"There are raps," he bethought him, "and raps."
And he said to Baldà, "Let it be so;
There is profit for thee and for me so;
Go and live in my yard,
And see that thou work for me nimbly and hard."

And he lives with the pope, does Baldà,
And he sleeps on straw pallet; but ah!
He gobbles like four men,
Yet he labours like seven or more men.
The sun is not up, but the work simply races;
The strip is all ploughed, and the nag in the traces;
All is bought and prepared, and the stove is well heated;
And Baldà bakes the egg and he shells it—they eat it;
And the popes heaps praise on Baldà,

And the daughter just pines for Baldà, and is sad;
And the little pope calls him *papa* ;
And he boils up the gruel, and dandles the lad.
But only the pope never blesses
Baldà with his love and caresses,
For he thinks all the while of the reckoning;
Times flies, and the hour of repayment is beckoning!
And scarce can he eat, drink, or sleep, for, alack,
Already he feels on his forehead the crack.
So he makes a clean breast to the popes.
And he asks where the last rag of hope is?
Now the woman is keen and quick-witted
And for any old trickery fitted,
And she says, "I have found us, my master,
A way to escape the disaster:
Some impossible job to Baldà now allot,
And command it be done to the very last jot;
So thy forehead will never be punished, I say,
And thou never shalt pay him, but send him away."

Then the heart of the pope is more cheerful
And his looks at Baldà are less fearful,
And he calls him: "Come here to me, do,
Baldà, my good workman and true!
Now listen: some devils have said
They will pay me a rent every year till I'm dead.
The income is all of the best; buy arrears
Have been due from those devils for three mortal years,
So when thou hast stuffed thyself full with the wheat,
Collect from those devils my quit-rent, complete."

It is idle to jar with the pope; so he,
Baldà, goes out and sits by the sea,
And there to twisting a rope he sets
And its further end in the sea he wets.
And an ancient fiend from the sea comes out:
"Baldà, why sneakest thou hereabout?"
"I mean with the rope the sea to wrinkle
And your cursed race to cramp and crinkle."
And the ancient then is grieved in mind:
"Oh why, oh why, art thou thus unkind?"
"Are ye asking *why*? and have not you
Forgotten the time when the rent was due?
But now, you dogs, we shall have our joke,
And you soon will find in your wheel a spoke."
"O dear Baldà, let the sea stop wrinkling,
And all the rent is thine in a twinkling.
I will send thee my grandson—wait awhile."
"He is easy enough," thinks Baldà, "to beguile!"

Then the messenger imp from the ocean darted,
And to mew like a famished kitten started.
"Good morrow, Baldà, my dear muzhik!
Now tell me, what is it, this rent you seek?
We never heard of your rent—that's flat;
Why, we devils have never had worries like that!

Yet take it, no matter!—on this condition,
For such is the judgment of our commission,
So that no grievance hereafter be—
The each of us run right round the sea,
And quickest shall have the whole of the tax.
Our folk, meanwhile, have made ready their sacks."
Then said Baldà, and he laughed so slily,
"Is this, my friend, the device so wily?
Shall the likes of thee in rivalry
Contend with the great Baldà, with *me*?
Art thou the foe who is sent to face me?
My Little Brother shall here replace me."

Then goes Baldà to the nearest copse;
Two hares he catches, in sack he pops,
And returns to the sea once more,
To the devilkin by the shore.
And he grips one hare by the ear;
"Thou shalt dance to our own balalaika, my dear.
Thou, devilkin, art but young and frail;
Dost thou strive with me? thou wilt only fail;
It is time and labour lost fir thee;

Outstrip my brother, and thou shalt see!
So, one, two, three, and away—now race him!"
Then off goes the imp, and the hare to chase him.
And the imp by the seashore coasted,
But the hare to the forest posted.
Now the imp has circled the seas about,
And he flies in panting, his tongue lolls out,
And his snout turns up, and he's thoroughly wet,
With his paw he towels away the sweat,
And he thinks he has settled Baldà. But there!
Baldà is stroking the brother-hare,
And repeating, "My own, my deary,
Now rest, my poor brother, for thou art weary!"
Then the imp of a heap was struck,
And tamely his tail through his legs he stuck;
At the brother-hare he glanced askew,
Said, "Wait, I will fetch the rent for you."
When he got to his granddad, "Too bad!" he said;
"Baldà—the young one—got right ahead."

Then the ancient fiend had a notion;
But Baldà made a noise and commotion,

And the ocean was vext,
And the waters were parted next,
And the imp slipt out: "Tis enough, muzhik;
We will send to you all the rent you seek.
But listen; dost thou behold this stick?
Now, choose thou a mark, and take thy pick;
And the one who the stick can farthest shoot, he
Shall have the whole of the rent for booty.
Why dost thou wait? why standest cowed?
Dost thou fear to sprain thy wrist?"—"Tis a cloud
Up there I await. I will toss thy stick up
Right in the cloud, and will start a kick-up
For you fiends!" And again he had won, had Baldà,
And the terrified imp told his grandpapa.
And Baldà again made the waters roar
And threatened the fiends with the rope once more;
And the imp popped up again; "Why dost fuss?
If thou wilt, thou shalt have all the rent from us."

"Nay, nay," says Baldà,
"I think it is my turn, ha ha!
Little enemy, now the conditions to make,
And to set thee a riddle to crack.
Let us see what thy strength is. Look there
At yonder gray mare:
I dare thee to lift her
And half a mile shift her.
So, carry that mare, and the rent is thine;
But carry her not, and the whole is mine."
And the poor little imp then and there
Crawled under the mare,
And there he lay lugging her,
And there he tugging her,
And he hoisted that mare for two paces; but falling
As he took the third, he dropt there sprawling.
Then says Baldà, "What avails to try,
Thou fool of an imp, with us to vie?
For thou, in thy arms thou couldst not rear her,
But see, between my legs I'll bear her."
And he mounted the mare, and galloped a mile,
And the dust eddied up; but the imp meanwhile
Ran scared to his grandad, and told him then
How Baldà was the winner again.

Then the devils, no help for it, rose and went
In a ring, and collected the whole of the rent,
And they loaded a sack
On Baldà, who made off with a kind of a quack.
And the pope when he sees him
Just skips up and flees him
And hides in the rear of his wife
And straddles, in fear of his life.
But Baldà hunts him out on the spot, and see!
Hands over the rent, and demands his fee.

Then the pope, poor old chap,
Put his pate up. At Rap
Number One, up he flew
To the celling. At Rap number Two
The pope, the poor wretch,
Lost his tongue and his speech.
And at Rap number Three he was battered,
And the old fellow's wits, they were shattered.
But Baldà, giving judgment, reproached him: "Too keen
Upon cheapness, my pope, thou hast been!"

1830

TALE OF THE DEAD PRINCESS AND THE SEVEN CHAMPIONS

TALE OF THE DEAD PRINCESS AND THE SEVEN CHAMPIONS

Once there was a king, who started
Journeying; from his queen he parted;
And she watched, a lonely thing,
At her window for her king.
Morn and eve she watched and waited;
Still the plain she contemplated
Till her eyes were sore, from white
Daybreak to the fall of night.
Never a sign of him, her lover!
All the earth is whitened over,
And the spinning snowstorms fall
On the plains; and that is all.
And her eyes she never raises
From the plains; nine months, she gazes.
—God, ere Christmas eve is morn,
Brings a gift: a girl is born.

In the morning early, homing
From afar where he was roaming,
Long awaited with desire,
Came at last the king and sire.
Just a look was his to capture;
But she could not bear the rapture;
Deeply, heavily she signed;
Near the hour of mass, she died.

Inconsolably, in seeming,
Flew a year of barren dreaming.
Kings are frail, other men;
Wedded was the king again.
Youthful was the queen he newly
Took to wife; I tell you truly,
She was shapely, white, and tall;
She was first, in wit and all;
Yet a captious, wilful spirit,
Proud, and envious of merit.
She for dowry of her own
Brought a looking-glass alone:
One of strange, peculiar fashion,
With the gift of conversation.
She was never kind or gay
When that mirror was away;
With it, pleasantly she jested;
Preened herself, and thus addressed it:
"Mirror, mirror, let me hear
Nothing but the truth, my dear!
Tell me, am I sweetest, fairest?"
Are my red and white the rarest?"
And the mirror still replies,
"Nay, be sure that none denies
Thou art sweetest, thou art fairest."
And the rosiest and rarest."
Then the queen in laughter breaks,
And her shoulders shrugs and shakes,
Snaps rejoicingly her fingers,
Winks, and blinks, and proudly lingers
Gazing, with a sidelong pace,
In the mirror at her face.

Silently, with none beholding,
Was the young princess unfolding
All the while; and grew, each hour,
Till at last the bud was flower.
Black her brows, and pale her features;
She was gentlest of all creatures.
Seeking her a husband, they
Found a prince, young Elisey.
Message came; the king consented,
And for portion he presented

Seven market-towns; may more,
Roomy chambers, seven score.

Now the queen has got upon her
All her finery, in honour
Of the marriage-eve; and now
She bespeaks the mirror: "Thou,
Tell me, am I sweetest, fairest?"
Are my red and white the rarest?"
But the mirror now replies:
"Thou art lovely, none denies;
But she sweetest, rosiest, fairest
Is the princess, and the rarest."

How the queen recoils and springs,
Brandishes her arms, and flings
Down the mirror, on it tramping.
With her booted heel, and stamping!
"Nasty, spiteful glass, I see
Thou art telling lies to me!

Would she rival me! I'll wholly
Soon dispose of such a folly!
What a creature she is grown!
Why, her mother, it is known,
When with child, on snow was gazing;
So—she's white!—Is that amazing?
Nay, but tell me: how should she
Overpass, in sweetness, me?
Journey all our kingdom over,
Though the whole wide world thou cover,
I'm the peerless one comfiest;
I of all am loveliest.
Tell me!" Still the glass said, "Fairer,
Rosier is the bride, and rarer."
So, no help! The lady next,
With the blackest envy vext,
Flings the glass beneath the benches,
Calls, amongst her chamber-wenches,
One Chernavka; bids her bear
Into some deep woody lair

That princess, and tightly bind her
Where the hungry wolves may find her
Underneath a pine alive
And devour her.
Now, to strive
With an angry dame is idle.
Not the Devil her can bridle.
Through the wood Chernavka passed
With the maid so far at last,
That the maid, the truth descrying,
Was for terror all but dying,
And besought her: "Precious one,
Say, what evil have I done?
Do not be my death; and, mind me,
Good and gracious shalt thou find me
On the day that I am queen."
But Chernavka love unseen
Bore her, neither bound nor slew her;
Left her free, made answer to her,
"God be with thee; never grieve";
Homeward then she took her leave.
"So, now tell me where the maid is,
That most beauteous of ladies,"
Asks the queen; the wench replies,
"In the wood alone she lies;
Beasts will catch and claw her, surely,
By the elbows lasht securely.
She will die the easier; less
Are her sufferings and distress."
Now the rumours ring and thicken
Of the lost princess; and stricken,
Pining for her, sits the king.
Elisey, petitioning
God with heart and soul, goes questing
On the highway, never resting
Till he find his promised wife
Young and fair, his very life.
But that young and lovely lady
Strayed about the forest shady,
Until daybreak threading it.
On a mansion then she lit,
Where a dog ran forward baying.

Then it ceased, and fell to playing;
Through the gate her way she found;
In the court was not a sound;
And the dog behind her wheeling
Fawned; and then the princess, stealing
Gently, mounted up the stair,
Grasped the door-ring hanging there,
And the door swung open lightly;
In a room illumined brightly
Next the princess found herself.
On the stove were tiles of delf
Made to lie on; pictures holy,
Oaken table, benches lowly
Laid with rugs, were there; and kind
Living people she would find,
Surely? – none to harm a woman.
Yet she noted nothing human.
Round the house the princess paced,
All things in good order placed,
To the Lord a taper kindled,
Lit the stove whose warmth had dwindled,
To an attic upward sped,
Laid her softly down to bed.
  Now the time to eat is coming;
Footsteps in the court are drumming.
Seven champions enter then,
Ruddy, bushy-whiskered men.
"All is wondrous bright and clean here,"
Says the eldest; "who hath been here?
Who hath set the room so straight?
Someone doth the hosts await.
Ay, but who? come forth and greet us!
Friendlike, honourably meet us!
Art thou aged? we will call

Thee our uncle, once for all.
If some ruddy lad or other,
Thou shalt have the name of brother.
If an ancient dame, then we
Will as mother honour thee.
If a comely maid thou prove thee,
Be our sister; we will love thee."
  And the princess issued thence,
Did her hosts due reverence,
Made a low, deep inclination,
Blushed, and faltered explanation
How beneath their roof she got

As a guest, though bidden not.
As the champions listened to her,
For a princess straight they knew her.
In a nook they set her there,
Served her with a pasty fair,
Poured a brimming cup, to stand
On a salver at her hand.
But the lady, with a sign,
Waved away the emerald wine;
Broke a corner of the pasty,
Nibbled at a morsel hasty;
But was wayworn, made request
For a bed, to take her rest.
Then the maiden they invited
To an upper room, well lighted,
And they left her there alone.
To her slumbers she is gone.
Like a flash the days go sliding;
Still the young princess is biding
In the wood; not wearisome

Is the seven champions' home.
Ere the dawn, in friendly rally
Out the brethren riding sally;
Take an airing, to let fly
At the grey-winged duck; or try,
All for sport, their sinews, dropping
Mounted Saracens, or lopping
Some broad-shouldered Tartar's pate;
Or from woods they extirpate
Pyatigorsk Circassians straying.
And the lady, still delaying,
Tarries in the room alone,
Keeping house while they are gone;
Makes all trim, prepares the dishes.
Never do they cross her wishes,
Never does she them gainsay.
Day in this wise follows day.
Now their hearts they all had given
Unto that dear maid. The seven
Brothers came one morn to her
Ere the sun was well astir.
Said the eldest: "We have told thee
How we all a sister hold thee,
All the seven; yet we all
Love thee; each one fine would call
Thee his wife, but that we may not.
So, for love of heaven, delay not;
Somehow set our hearts at rest;
Be the wife of one—the best,
To the six a sister loving.
Why that headshake unapproving?
Wilt not have us? Is the ware
Not for purchase—all too rare?"
"Lads of honour! Ye, none others,"
Said she, "are my own, own brothers.
If I lie, may God command
That I perish where I stand;
Know ye then, that I am plighted;
What shall serve? I cannot right it.
Ye are equal in mine eyes;
All are valiant, all are wise;
Each one hath my love sincerest;

Палех · 1979 г.
Н. Лопатин.

But another still is dearest;
I must his for ever be;
Elisey, the prince, is he."
Mute they stood; and as she ended,
Scratched their necks: "Be not offended!
Asking, surely, is no sin";
And the eldest bowed : "We win
Pardon? Is it so?—then say not
In excuse one word."
"I may not
Chide you," soft the answer came;
"For my *No* I'm not to blame."
Then they did meet reverence to her;
Quietly retired each wooer;
Lived their old lives, every one,
All in peace and unison.
But the wicked queen, still fretting,
Not forgiving or forgetting,
On the princess thought, and long
Chafed in anger at the wrong
Done her by the glass, and pouted.
But she threw her arms about it
In the end, and sat her down
Facing it; forgot to frown,
And once more began to preen her;
Said, with smiling day demeanour,
"Mirror, greetings! Let me hear
Nothing but the truth, my dear;
Tell me, am I sweetest, fairest?
Are my red and white the rarest?"
And the mirror, it replies,
"Thou art lovely, none denies.
Yet in oakwoods green and shady,
All unnoted lives a lady,
Housed with seven champions; now,
She is sweeter far than thou."
Then the queen in wrath flew at her;
"Thou, Chernavka, in this matter
Durst thou trick me?"—To the rest,
Point by point, the wench confessed.
And that evil queen did warn her
That a collar might adorn her
Set with spikes! "Now die," she saith,
"Or the princess do to death."
Once the young princess, who waited
For her brothers dear belated,
At her window spun; and there
Suddenly below the star
Heard the angry house-dog growling.
There, within the court, was prowling
Just a nun who begged for food
While with crutch the dog she shooed.
Down the lady called, "Good mother,
I will scare him; stop the pother,
Only wait, and thou wilt see

What I'm bringing down to thee."
But the nun was heard replying,
"Ah, my child, I'm near to dying,
Worried by thy hateful cur;
Watch him, raising all the stir!
Come, come out and help me, darling!"
But the dog, who still was snarling
When the princess tried to go
With a loaf, and stept below,
Pushed between her feet, nor let her
Reach the crone, who moved and met her.
At the crone he still would bay,
And no woodland beast of prey
Could have flown at her more madly.
Was it strange?
"He's slept so badly!
Look, and catch!" the princess said,
As she tossed her out the bread.
And the crone, when she had caught it,
Cried her thanks to her who brought it:
"May God bless thee! Now, to match,
Here is something for thee: catch!"
And a pippin straight she tosses,
Juicy, fresh, with golden glosses,
To the princess. How the hound
Whimpers, springing from the ground!
—Clap! With both her hands
she snatches
And the pippin deftly catches.
"Say your grace, and eat the prime
Pippin; it will kill the time,
Dearest!" Thus the beldame crying

Bows and vanishes. But flying
With the princess to the stair
Fiercely howls the dog, and there
Sadly looks upon her, making
As his doggish heart were aching
And as though he would command
"Drop the thing!" Her gentle hand

Ruffles, pats him and caresses:
"Falcon, something thee distresses?
Down!" Within her room she passed,
Quietly the door made fast,
By her yarn at window sitting,
Waiting for her hosts; but flitting
Towards her pippin were her eyes.

Ripe and sappy was the prize,
Fresh and fragrant as a posy,
And as golden as a rosy,
As if honey-filled; and she
Through the rind the pips could see.
First she thought that eat she would not
Till the meal; but wait she could not:
To her crimson lips the fruit,
Clasped in either hand, she put.
Nibble upon nibble followed,
And a morsel next she swallowed...

Suddenly the snowy hands
Of our dear one flag; she stands
Reeling, and her breath is stopping,
And the ruddy fruit is dropping,
And she rolls her eyes, and falls
By the ikons on the walls
Headlong to the bench, and by it
Lies, immovable and quiet.

And the brethren, who had made
Some courageous, cunning raid,
Now were trooping homeward proudly.
But the house-dog, yelping loudly,
Ran to meet them, showed the way
To the court. "Bad luck to-day!"
Said the brethren, "some disaster
Here is certain." Rushing faster,
Springing in, they looked, and groaned.
And the dog, he barked and moaned,
Fiercely at the pippin flying,
Gulped it down, and tumbled dying,
And expired. Behold, the bait
Was with poison saturate.

Then the brethren bow before her,
In their deepest soul deplore her;
Lift her from the bench, array her
For her burial, but survey her
Wavering—the lady so
Tranquil lay and fresh, as though
Sleep's own plumes were her enwreathing,
And they almost thought her breathing.
So three days they watched; but she

Rose not, slumbering peaceably.
Then the mournful rites they paid her;
In a crystal coffin laid her,
And that young princess in state
All the band conveyed, to wait
On a mountain, named Deserted.
Lofty pillars they inserted
For her coffin, six in all,
At the midnight hour; withal
Safe with iron chains they nailed it;
With a grating round they railed it;
And before their sister dead
Earthward bent; the eldest said:

Coffined there, may sleep bestrew thee.
Swiftly malice quenched and slew thee;
Earth thy beauty still doth gain;
Heaven thy soul must entertain.
Best beloved we esteemed thee.
Cherished thee, and sweetest deemed thee.
No man had thee for his own;
Thou wert for the grave alone.

But the wicked queen was watching
For good news that day, and catching
Secretly her glass, she made
Question as of old, and said,
"Tell me, am I sweetest, fairest?
Are my red and white the rarest?"
In her ear the glass replies,
"Such thou art; and none denies
Thou art sweetest, rosiest, fairest
Of all women, and the rarest."
Seeking still his promised bride
Over all the earth must ride
Elisey. But nought availing
Are his bitter tears and wailing.
He may ask of whom he will,
None to answer has the skill;
In his face they laugh and flout him,
Or they show their backs and scout him.
Then at last the warrior turned
To the Sun, who redly burned:
"Sun, our luminary, pacing
Yearlong round the skies, and chasing
With warm spring the winter snow,
Seeing all men here below,
In the wide world hast thou ever
Seen a young princess? ah, never,
Surely, wilt thou grudge reply:
Her affianced man am I."
"None, dear youth, have I beholden,"
Said the ruddy sun and golden.
"Is she numbered with the dead?
Yet my neighbour-Moon," he said,
"Somewhere may have met and faced her,
Or by footprints may have traced her."
Elisey, whose heart was sick,
Waited till the night fell thick;
Saw the Moon new-risen, and hailed her;
With entreaty thus assailed her:
"Moon, thou Moon, good friend of mine,
Horned and gilded, who dost shine
In the misty deeps upblazing,
Round of face, and brightly gazing,
Thou whom all the stars survey
Loving still thy wonted way,
In the wide world hast thou ever
Marked a young princess? ah, never,
Surely, wilt thou grudge reply!
Her affianced man am I."

"Brother," said the Moon serenely,
"I have marked no maiden queenly.
Only in my turn I dwell
At my post as sentinel.
Doubtless, while she past was flying
I had gone." And he was crying,
"Ah, the pity of it!" "Nay,"
Then the clear Moon added, "stay;
For the Wind will help thee, lover,
And may give thee tidings of her;
Therefore get thee to him now.
So, farewell; and fret not thou."

Then he plucked up heart, and speeding
To the Wind, began his pleading:
"Wind, O Wind, so strong and proud,
Chaser of flocks of cloud,
Stirrer of the azure ocean,
Ranging space in airy motion,
Going in the fear of none
Saving the Lord God alone,
In the wide world hast thou ever
Marked a young princess? ah, never,
Surely, wilt thou grudge reply;
Her affianced man am I."

№ 683 с. Палех. 1996 г
Шатохина Ж. ©

Said the Storm-Wind: "Tarry: yonder,
Past where quiet waters wander,
Is a lofty mountain, where
Lies a hole profound; and there
Swings within that hole abysmal,
Chained to pillars, in a dismal
Mirk, a crystal coffin; round
All that barren place are found
No man's tracks; the coffin laden
Is with her, thy plighted maiden."
Then the Wind sped on. But he
Gave one sob, and, fain to see
Once again his lady plighted
In her beauty, went, and lighted
On that barren place. Behold,
Now a craggy mountain bold
Towers before him, and around it
Lies a barren land to bound it.
Swiftly, swiftly doth he go
To an entry dark below.
There, in blackness melancholy
Swings a crystal coffin slowly;
Crystal-coffined, lies she deep,
His princess, in endless sleep.
Then with all his might he battered
At his dear one's coffin. Shattered
Suddenly, the coffin broke;
Suddenly the maid awoke;
Looked with wandering eyes around her,
Swayed above the chains that bound her,
Heaved a mighty sigh, and said
"See how long I've laid abed!"

From the coffin she is creeping;
Ah, for joy they both are weeping!
Now he lifts the maid away
Out of darkness into day
And the two are homeward faring,
Happy, friendly talk are sharing.

Quickly round the tidings ring,
"Saved—the daughter of the king!"
Idly, that same hour, was waiting
The bad stepdame, and debating
With her glass at home; so ran
Converse, as the queen began:

"Am I not the sweetest, fairest?
Are my red and white the rarest?"
In her ear the glass replies,
"Thou art lovely, none denies,
But the sweetest, rosiest, fairest
Is the princess, and the rarest."
Up the wicked stepdame leapt,
To the floor the glass she swept
Broken, and rushed out, and straightway
Met the princess in the gateway.
Sick of soul, discomfited
Was that queen, and there fell dead.
Scarce to earth had she been carried,
They made ready to be married.
Then was wedded Elisey
To his bride with no delay.

Never, since the world's creation,
Saw man such a celebration.
I drank beer, drank mead, and yet
Hardly were my whiskers wet.

1833

„Сказка

царевне и семи богатырях"
с. Палех. 1992г.

Из произв. А.С. Пушкина. сказка о рыбаке и рыбке.
село Палех. 1994 года И. Зубков.

TALE OF THE FISHERMAN AND THE LITTLE FISH

TALE OF THE FISHERMAN AND THE LITTLE FISH

An old man, his old woman with him,
Lived close by the dark blue ocean.
In a shaky mud hut they were living
For just thirty-three years exactly.
The old man with his net would go fishing,
And her yarn the dame would be spinning.
Once he cast his net in the ocean,
And the net came up with mud only.
When he cast out his net the next time
The net came up just with seaweed.
And he cast his net for the third time,
And the net, with a fish it came up,
Not a common fish, but a golden.
Then the golden fish asks for mercy,
Speaking with the voice of a mortal:
"Let me go, old man, into the ocean;
A costly ransom I will give thee;

My ransom is whatever thou wishest."
The old man marvelled, he was frightened;
Three and thirty years he had been fishing
And never had he heard of a fish talking.
And the golden fish, he released it,
Saying to it a word of kindness:
"Golden fish, now may God be with thee!
For I have no need of the ransom.
So depart thou into the blue ocean,
A-roaming by thyself in freedom."

The old man, to his dame returning,
Related to her the mighty marvel:
"I was just a-catching a fish this morning,
Not a common fish, but a golden,
And the fish, she spoke to me in Russian;
She begged to go home to the blue ocean,
And ransomed herself with a costly payment:
I might wish for what I like for ransom!
But I did not dare to take the ransom,
So let her go in the blue ocean."
The old man from his dame got a rating:
"A simpleton art thou and a blockhead;
Not able to take the fish's ransom!

Why, a trough thou mightst have taken from her;
For ours is all broken and battered."

Then he went to the dark blue ocean,
And saw the ocean a little ruffled;
And to the golden fish he shouted,
And the fish swam up to him, and asked him,
"What mayst thou be wanting, old fellow?"
The old man answered her, bowing,
"Have pity, O my fish, my princess!
My old woman has rated me soundly;
I am old, she gives me no quiet;
For she is wanting a trough, a new one,
And ours is all broken and battered."
And the golden fish gave him answer:
"Begone, and grieve not; Got be with thee.
For ye shall have your trough, a new one."

Then back to his dame went the old man.
By the dame was a trough, a new one.
But the dame, she scolds worse then ever:
"A simpleton art thou and a blockhead!
Blockhead, just a trough for thy begging!
There is little *truck* in a *trough,** now!
Get thee back to the fish, thou blockhead;
Bow to her, beg of her a cottage."

---

* Play, in the original, on *koryto* (through) and *koryst'* (profit).

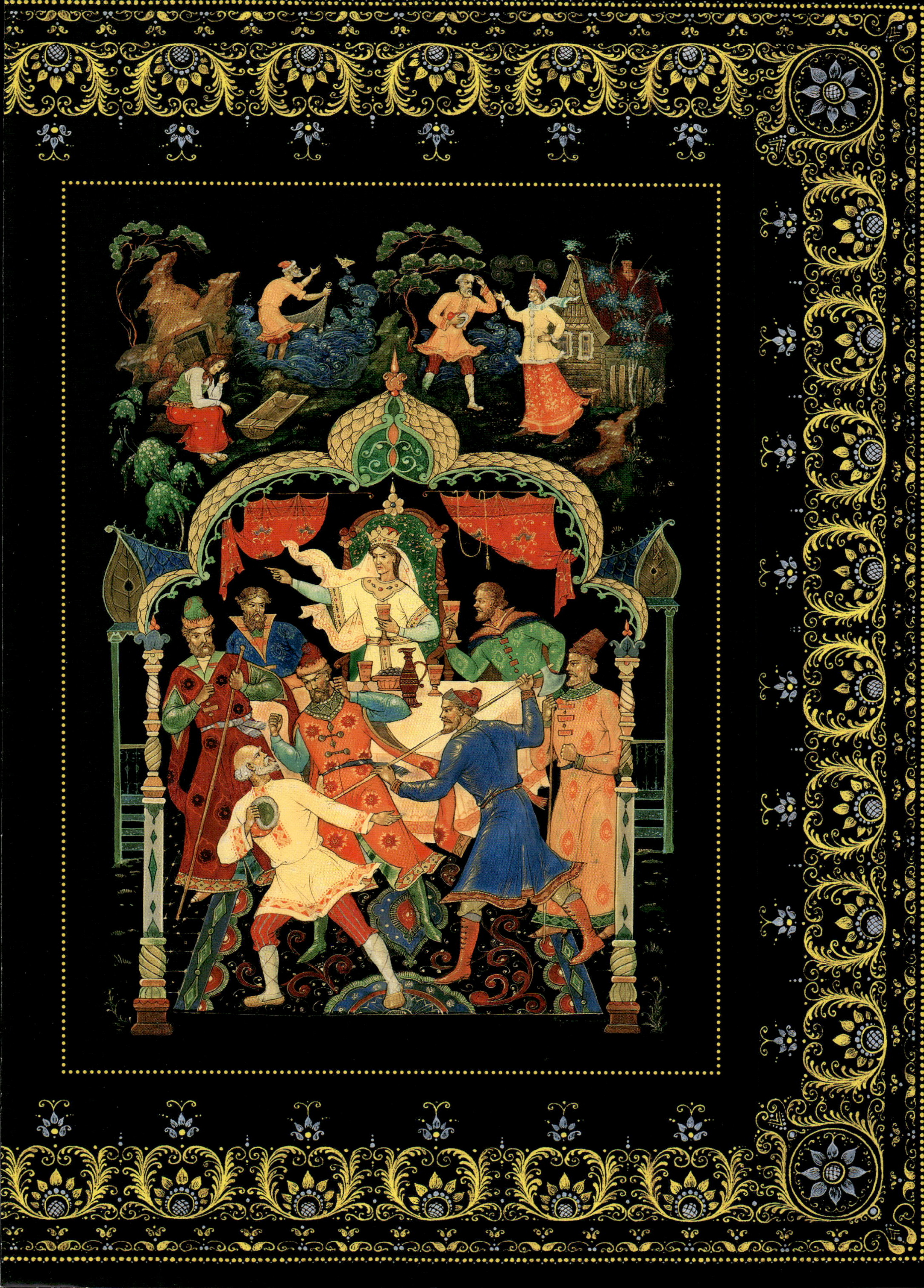

Then he went to the dark blue ocean
(And the dark blue ocean was troubled)
And to the golden fish he shouted,
And the fish swam up to him, and asked him,
"What mayst thou be wanting, old fellow?"
The old man answered her, bowing:
"Have pity, O my fish, my princess!
For my dame is scolding more than ever;
I am old, she gives me no quiet;
And the old shrew asks for a cottage."
And the golden fish gave him answer,
"Begone, and grieve not; God be with thee;
Be it so; ye shall have your cottage."

He went to his hut; it had been earthen;
But the earthen hut had all vanished.
Before him is a cottage, with attic,
With a chimney all of brick and whitened,
And the gate is made of oaken planking,
The old woman sits there at the window
And mightily she abuses her husband:
"Thou simpleton and perfect blockhead!

Simpleton, thou hast begged a cottage!
Back to the fish, and bow before her;
I would not be a vulgar peasant,
But would be a lady of position."

Then he went to the dark blue ocean
(The blue ocean was disquieted)
And to the golden fish he shouted,
And the fish swam up to him, asking,
"What mayst thou be wanting, old fellow?"
The old man answered her, bowing:
"Have pity, O my fish, princess!
My old woman is fooling worse than ever;
I am old, she gives me no quiet;
She would not be a peasant any longer,
She would be a lady of position."
And the golden fish gave him answer,
"Begone, and grieve not; God be with thee."

Then back to his dame went the old man.
What beholds he? A lofty mansion!
On the stairway stands his old woman
In a costly warm coat of sables,
On her crown a brocaded head-dress.
And her neck, with pearls it is loaded;
On her hands are rings, which are golden;
On her feet are shoes, which are crimson.
Diligent servants are before her;
She beats them, she tweaks them by the forelock.
The old man said to his old woman
"Greeting, madam lady and mistress!
Now perhaps thy soul is contented."
And the old woman squalled out at him
And sent him to the stable to serve there.

So a week goes by, and another.
The old woman is fooling more than ever;
Yet again to the fish she sends him:
"Back to the fish, and bow before her;
I would not be a lady of position;
I want to be a ruler and an empress."
The old man was in terror, he entreated:

"Old woman, hast thou feasted upon henbane?
How to walk, and how to talk, thou hast forgotten;
Thou wilt set the whole empire laughing."

The old woman was angrier than ever
And on the cheek she cuffed her husband:
"Peasant, dar'st thou to argue with me,
With me, lady of position?
Get thee to the sea—and on my honour,
If thou dost not, shalt be taken willy-nilly."
The old man made off to the ocean
(The blue ocean had darkened over)
And to the golden fish he shouted,
And the fish swam up to him, asking,
"What mayst thou be wanting, old fellow?"
The old man answered her, bowing:
"Have pity, O my fish, my princess!
Again my old woman is rebelling;
Cares no more to be lady of position,
Wants to be a ruler and an empress."
And the golden fish gave him answer,
"Begone, and grieve not; God be with thee;
Good! thy old woman shall be empress."

Then back to his dame went the old man.
Lo, before him an imperial palace!

In the palace he sees his old woman
Sitting at the table, an empress;
Her servants are boyars and nobles,
And wine from overseas they pour her;
Gingerbread, all stamped, she is eating.
And a dread bodyguard surrounds her,
They have got axes on their shoulders.
When the old man saw them, he was frightened,
Bowed at the feet of the old woman,
Saying, "I bid thee hail, dread empress!
Now perhaps thy soul is contented."
The old woman never looked at him,
Just bade them drive him from her presence.
Then ran up the boyars and nobles,
And they scruffed the old fellow forwards,
And up ran the guard at the doorway,
All but chopping him with their axes.
And the common people bemocked him:
"Thou deservest it, thou boorish ancient!
Be instructed, thou boor, hereafter,
Do not sit in the sledges of others!"
So the week goes by, and the next one;
The old woman is fooling more than ever.
She sends her courtiers to her husband,

They hunt out the old man and bring him.
And the dame, she says to her old man:
"Back to the fish, and bow before her;
I would not be ruler and an empress,
I would fain of the sea be sovereign,
So as to live in the sea, the Ocean,
So that the golden fish may serve me,
And go as my messenger on errands."
And the old man, he durst not oppose her,
Durst not utter a word to cross her.
Now he goes to the dark blue ocean,
He looks—on the sea is a black tempest;
So swollen are the angry billows,
So rush they, such a roar are they raising.
And to the golden fish he shouted,
And the fish swam up to him, asking,
"What mayst thou be wanting, old fellow?"
The old man answered her, bowing,
"Have pity, O my fish, my princess!
How deal with her, my dammed old
woman?
She wants no longer to be empress,
She wants of the sea to be sovereign,
So as to live in the sea, the Ocean,
That *thou* thyself mayst be her servant
And be her messenger on errands."
But the fish, not a word she uttered,
She just plashed with her tail in the water
And went off in the depths of ocean.
Long by ocean he awaited an answer
In vain—and went back to his old woman.
See! The old mud hut is before him;
His old woman sits on the threshold,
And before her is a trough in flinders.

1833

CONTENTS

PUSHKIN'S FAIRY TALES. PALEKH PAINTING

Medny Vsadnik Trading House Publishers, 2017
Designed by Denis Lazarev
Photographs by Pavel Demidov and Oleg Trubsky

Illustrations by Palekh Artists:
Oleg An, Andrei Arapov, Svetlana Baikina, Grigory Bakanov, Ivan Bakanov, Serguei Bakhirev, Alexander Baranov, Pavel Bazhenov, Roman Belousov, Valentina Belozerova (Russina), Alexander Blokhin, Konstantin Bokarev, Valery Bokarev, Valery Bolshakov, Alexander Borunov, Vladimir Buldakov, Nathalia Buldakova, Vladimir Bushkov, Dmitry Butorin, Aristarkh Dydykin, Stepan Gavrilov, Ivan Golikov, Nikolai Golikov, Antonina Ivanova, Serguei Kalinin, Ivan Kamanin, Serguei Kamanin, Valentin Khodov, Vladimir Kholmov, Nadezhda Khomyakova, Alexander Klipov, Alexei Kochupalov, Lubov Kortikova, Alexander Kotukhin, Vladimir Kotukhin, Anna Kotukhina, Nadezhda Kovach, Victor Krivtsov, Yury Krysenkov, Alexander Kurkin, Trofim Liatov, Nikolai Lopatin, Nina Lopatina, Ivan Markichev, Irina Mayevskya, Georgy Mironov, Galina Mochalina, Vitaly Mukhin, Evguenia Nebogatova, Alexander Nikolaev, Victor Panin, Nikolai Paramonov, Victor Paramonov, Svetlana Paramonova, V. Pashkova, Evguenia Shatokhina, Mikhail Shishkov, Vasily Skalozub, Vladimir Smirnov, Alexander Terekhin, Olga Tsiganova, Dmitry Urban, Nathalia Urban, Ivan Vakurov, Nikolai Vakurov, Alexei Vatagin, Serguei Velikanov, Yuri Vinogradov, Larisa Viuguina, Irina Yablokova, Boris Yermolaev, Valery Yuskov, Alexei Zaitsev, Victor Zhegalov, Nikolai Zimin, Nikolai Zinoviev, Victor Zolotarev, Ivan Zubkov, Tamara Zubkova, Galina Zykova

Editor by Irina Lvova
Computer design by Svetlana Bashun
Colour correction by Viacheslav Bykovski, Vladimir Kniazev, Alexander Miagkov

Изготовитель
Торговый дом «Медный всадник». www.mvsadnik.ru. Тел./факс (812) 309-59-61
192029, Россия, Санкт-Петербург, пр. Обуховской Обороны, д. 95, корп. 2